SEEKERS OF MEANING

SEEKERS OF

MEANING

*Baby Boomers, Judaism,
and the Pursuit of*
HEALTHY AGING

Richard F. Address

URJ PRESS

New York, New York

Library of Congress Cataloging-in-Publishcation Data

Addressm, Richar F.

Seekers of meaning : baby boomers, Judaism, and the pursuit of healthy aging / Richard F. Address.

p. cm.

Includes bibliographical references.

ISBN 978-0-8074-1226-8

1. Aging—Religious aspects—Judaism.   2. Older Jews—Religious life.   3. Older Jews—Identification.   4. Identification (Religion)   6. Spiritual life—Judaism.
I. Title.

BM540.A35A33 2011

296.7084´6—dc23

2011037194

Every attempt has been made to obtain permission to reprint previously published material. The publisher gratefully acknowledges the following for permission to reprint previously published material:

CCAR PRESS: "Birth Is a Beginning" by Alvin Fine, from *Gates of Repentance*, edited by Chaim Stern, © 1978 by Central Conference of American Rabbis. All rights reserved. Used by permission.

KTAV PUBLISHING HOUSE: "Holding On and Letting Go" from *In God's Mirror* by Harold M. Schulweis, © 1990. Used with permission of Ktav Publishing House, Inc.

METRO-GOLDWYN-MAYER STUDIOS: *Crimes and Misdemeanors* © 1989 Orion Pictures Corporation. All rights reserved. Courtesy of MGM Media Licensing.

All quotes from the Torah come from *The Torah: A Modern Commentary*, revised edition, edited by W. Gunther Plaut (New York: URJ Press, 2005). The quotes from Ecclesiastes come from *The Tanakh: A New Translation of the Holy Scriptures* (Philadelphia: Jewish Publication Society, 1985).

For permission to reprint, please contact:
URJ Press
633 Third Avenue
New York, NY 10017-6778
(212) 650-4120
press@urj.org

Printed on acid-free paper

Copyright © 2012 by URJ Press

Manufactured in the United States of America

10 9 8 7 6 5 4 3 2 1

To my parents

Martin Address, z"l

Jeanette Address, z"l

and to my friend

Rabbi Lawrence "Jake" Jackofsky, z"l

Contents ———————————————

Preface ——————

O N A BLUSTERY WINTER SUNDAY NOT TOO LONG ago, I sat with a group of my contemporaries—baby boomers, men and women in their fifties and early sixties—discussing our spiritual journeys and the growing sense that we were all at or entering a stage of life filled with challenges and uncertainty, but also the potential for communal engagement and personal creativity. The discussion was one of many I have held with members of synagogues on the aging of baby boomers and how this group relates to Jewish life. One congregant, Hope, spoke of the delicate balance of her life; she was, as is quite typical, juggling advancing in her career, raising a teenager about to leave for college, and caring for elderly parents. Hope and her husband were active members of their suburban congregation. Yet when the conversation turned to the spiritual sustenance that they received, there was an uncomfortable lull. As the discussion continued, Jessica commented on her own spiritual journey and personal search, which had become more important in recent years as she became more aware of her own aging. She noted that while she remained committed to her congregation, "something had always been missing for me." Like many others, her journey had taken her to New Age lectures and books, Buddhism, Jewish renewal classes, and interfaith spirituality and dialogue groups. Hope spoke of the push-pull dance in which so many of us are now engaged, the tension between the congregation that gave birth to her spiritual journey and her own need to find a sense of spiritual completeness as she ages: "While my spiritual journey has taken me many places, I plan to continue it at my synagogue, in addition to pursuing whatever else I feel can enhance my spirituality." Roseanne, a woman active for years both in her community and with national Jewish organizations, was even more blunt: "I don't think that Judaism plays any role in my concerns or how I am approaching this time of my life. In fact, if I were honest, I'd say that the observances mean less. I sit in services and don't have the grand sense of God I used to have when I was younger. I have a strong sense of community, but not God. Maybe I need to spend more time, sort of, back to basics!"

Many of us, myself included, understand what Hope and Roseanne are saying. We are spiritually homeless, searching for something—not material, but a feeling, a sense of self that can reaffirm the mystery of being alive. By the time we reach our late fifties, we have lived enough to recognize the challenges that life holds for us, and our accumulated experience has begun to alter our worldview. At another focus group, Marshall spoke to this when he commented that "as the markers of who we are in our work lives fall away in importance (our job, material things, etc.), and as our children grow and we watch our own parents age, care for them, and experience their death, these changes have caused an evolution in my own thinking process and has reordered my priorities. . . . It is important to search for one's own core ethics and personal values which inform and shape our own lives. This type of thinking doesn't take place in one's thirties and forties—and I find maturity very comforting."

Welcome to the world of the aging Jewish baby boomer; challenged by the need to be part of an existing community, yet feeling free to experiment with new, more personal forms of Jewish expression. Looking ahead at years if not decades of life still to live, they ask, How can Judaism provide a source of support, caring, and guidance for the next stage of my life? Is there a foundation on which to base this search, or must I make it up as I go along? As the baby boom generation ages, many of its members are uncertain about their own future, their Jewish identity, and the role that the Jewish community should play in their lives. The contemporary Jewish community is being presented with a unique challenge and opportunity to respond to the spiritual search for meaning now unfolding as the baby boomers age. This search may take the form of new and innovative expressions of Judaism. Yet to ignore this challenge is to court irrelevancy. A 2009 study by David M. Elcott, Ph.D., of the Berman Jewish Policy Archive at New York University, titled "Baby Boomers, Public Service and Minority Communities: A Case Study of the Jewish Community in the United States" and prepared in conjunction with Civic Ventures, looked at attitudes among members of the Jewish community regarding meaningful work—paid and volunteer—that could engage baby boomers as they age. The study showed that baby boomers, long the stalwarts of Jewish communal life, are drifting away from locating their own sense of meaning within the Jewish community. Uncertainty regarding their aging seems to add to a sense of uncertainty regarding Jewish identity. Likewise, the report indicated that the Jewish community itself has yet to understand the impact of this revolution in longevity. Professor Steven M. Cohen, who directs the Berman Jewish Policy Archive, called attention to this:

> But not only are Jews (as others) living longer, they are living in an age of meaning-seeking, with the interest and wherewithal to make living a life of meaning an ultimate and reasonably obtainable objective for any point in their lives. As such, this aging yet largely healthy generation of American Jews poses a challenge (and opportunity) to a society and community that is as yet unprepared for the totally new policy and planning possibilities that loom in the near future. (Steven M. Cohen 2010, p. 2)

Judaism in North America is changing right before our eyes. The engine that is driving much of this transition is the growing spiritual concerns of the baby boom generation as they seek a sense of meaning and purpose. The 2001 National Jewish Population Survey noted that almost 20 percent of the Jewish population of the United States was age sixty-five and older. Now, a decade later, that number is swelling as members of the first wave of the baby boom generation (people born between 1945 and the early 1960s) enters their sixties. According to U.S. government statistics, as of January 1, 2011, one person in the country was turning sixty-five every eight seconds. Thanks to advances in medical technology and a greater sensitivity to issues of health, nutrition, and exercise, boomers now can hope for and expect decades more of life. Time is both friend and foe. What shall we do with this "gift" of time and longevity? We assume, and hope, that this time will be spent in health and vitality. Yet, what happens when that time is filled with chronic illness and loss of independence? Where and how will our congregations and our own relationship to Judaism respond to this swelling cohort of older adults when, for much of the community, the focus continues to be on youth?

What new challenges will emerge? As we live longer, so too are our parents. The new life stage of caregiver is one in which a large proportion of us are actively engaged. At the same time, many of us are still very involved with our own children and, given the economic uncertainties that surround so many, we continue to be concerned about our own retirement nest eggs. So, we forestall retirement as the demands of our multigenerational families define so much of what we do. And in the middle of this journey, we begin to see friends being overwhelmed with illness and, if we are so blessed, given the opportunity to enter another life stage, that of grandparent. Time seems to speed up and we look for a sense of rootedness and security so as not to lose our own sense of self. Didn't someone tell us years ago that this time in our lives was going to be "our" time? If so, why are we working so hard and juggling so much? How can we bring a sense of meaning and purpose to this time? Can Judaism, in its richness, offer us a guide to help navigate these new life stages?

The purpose of this book is to provide a foundation for that search, based on what I call the "theology of relationships." This is a belief that the most powerful and important aspects of our lives are the relationships that we have, and that, as we age, those relationships gain greater importance and are the source of our own search for meaning. Relationships help give our lives texture and definition, as well as providing a sense of validation, support, caring, and purpose. They are the antidote to our fear of loneliness. The theology of relationships is based on a series of texts from the Torah that empower us and give us permission to continually grow as individuals and as a community. They are texts that reinforce the centrality of being with others and in relationship to others, for those connections can be the source of our own growth and health.

Judaism itself is a community-based religious civilization. You cannot be Jewish by yourself. You need people, community, and relationships. It is a belief system that supports inclusion and openness, and, in this age of transition, never has this belief been more crucial. The belief in the primacy of relationships emanates from the very beginning of the Torah. Our primary, fundamental relationship is with God. Genesis 1, the first of the texts we will study, spells this out for us clearly, as it reminds us that we are created "in the image of God" (*b'tzelem Elohim*). The very first relationship we have is with God, and this relationship serves as a model for how we should relate to others. As we shall see later on, it also forms the foundation on which everything else is based.

Intrinsic to the idea of being *b'tzelem Elohim* is the idea that we are, by the mere fact that we exist, unique. We are also driven, in a fundamental way, to seek out meaning through relationships with others. Indeed, the motivation for this basic drive can be found in the twin emotions of love and loneliness. We seek community so that we are not alone. We translate that desire for community and love to the world through the embrace of mitzvot, the sacred obligations that define us as a people, for in reaching out to the world, we find meaning for our own selves. This desire to seek meaning, especially as we age, is a direct response to the central call of our second text, Genesis 3. God calls us to answer our tradition's first question: *Ayecha?* Where are you? As we become more aware of our own mortality, the desire to find an answer to God's question becomes more important.

In every discussion I've had with baby boomers, a powerful sense emerges that so much is changing: not only the world around us, but our own selves. For some of us, it is first apparent when we stumble into the bathroom in the middle of the night, turn on the light, look at the reflection in the mirror, and ask, "Who are you and where did you come from?" Change is part of who we are, and the way we deal with it—whether we accept and welcome it or fight it tooth and nail—has much to say about how we age and how we live our lives. Change is sometimes thrust upon us, as when Abraham is told to "go forth" in the Torah portion *Lech l'cha* (Genesis 12, our third text), and it is sometimes the result of powerful forces within ourselves and our society with which we grapple.

Judaism teaches us that the number of years we have has no bearing on the number of experiences that are open to us. Our tradition gives us permission to seek new experiences, self-definitions, and, at times, lives. Those changes may involve wrestling with our very souls, as Jacob did in Genesis 32, the fourth text we will explore. It is often painful—spiritually, psychologically, and physically—to change who we are and how we see ourselves. Yet it is sometimes necessary to do so in order to avoid stagnation, even death of the soul. Thus, we are taught that, as we age, we need not fear the changes in ourselves, or how others see us, for we are constantly engaged in trying to determine our own unique answer to God's *ayecha*.

The problem for many of us is, of course, what we mean by *God*. In our fifth text, Exodus 3, we are given permission to engage in a lifelong dialogue regarding our relationship with and definition of God; this is one of the great gifts of our tradition. This dialogue is of special significance as we age, as our experiences temper and give definition to our lives and we try to forge a legacy that we can leave to our children and grandchildren. We want a religious expression that reflects a God concept that speaks to our lives and our experiences, not one that was based on who we were when we became bar or bat mitzvah. We want to be part of something beyond our own selves.

The sixth text behind the theology of relationships, Leviticus 19, helps define the changes and transitions that now lie before us. It teaches that life must be made holy. Holiness is the substance that binds us together in relationship. It is the often fragile bond that unites parents and children in caregiving and is the movement, like a flower arching toward the sun, of humankind to do good, to model what we perceive to be God. Yet, choosing a life of holiness often involves making decisions that are not clear cut. One of the gifts of growing older is understanding the value and importance of gray. Rarely are the choices we have to make a matter of black or white. Rather, they contain shades of gray. How we make decisions and what we decide to do determine the quality and character of our lives. Herein lies one of the values of reminiscing and the desire to create a lasting and sacred legacy for those who come after us. The Jewish tradition's concept of the ethical will is a reflection of the powerful lessons we can learn from examining the way in which people have made their choices and lived their lives before us.

Deuteronomy 30, the final text in our study, reinforces the understanding that we are defined by the choices we make and therefore we are responsible for what and how we choose. This is perhaps one of the greatest gifts of our tradition. It reminds us that we are responsible for the lives we live. There are many aspects of our lives over which we have no control. Yet there are so many aspects of life that, little by little, choice by choice, determine who we become and, in many ways, how we are remembered. We seek meaning through the choices we make; thus the call of Deuteronomy 30 to "choose life" becomes even more powerful as we grow older. Life remains our most precious and fragile gift. Now, blessed with the opportunity to create and be engaged in the search for meaning in our longevity, the texts of our tradition can take on even more powerful relevance in our own journeys to meaning and purpose.

MUCH OF THE GROUNDWORK FOR THIS BOOK WAS LAID in the development and programming of the project on Sacred Aging for the Union for Reform Judaism's Department of Jewish Family Concerns. The project, which included pilot programs in congregations and a survey of their members, grew out of an awareness of the changing demographics of the contemporary Jewish community. In discussions with baby boomers across North America, what emerged was a portrait of a generation that was searching for a more intimate and personal relationship with Judaism. In our work, we discovered that most congregations were unprepared for the revolution in aging. Slowly we observed the gradual rise in baby boomers leaving congregations because they felt that there was little in congregational life that addressed the particular needs and challenges of their new longevity. In a very real way, what participants in these discussions and surveys were saying is that they wanted their congregations and their Jewish community to help them navigate the changes and transitions that are now defining so much of life. The questions that emerged from the project were profound: What does it mean to have decades of life remaining after so many years focused on child rearing and work? How can my Judaism guide me in caregiving for my parents or my spouse? What guidance can this tradition give me if, God forbid, I must make a decision that could mean the end of a loved one's life due to illness? How can I keep my relationship with my spouse alive and "sacred"? How can I make the time I have before me meaningful and purposeful? What will my legacy be, what will my life mean, and what message can I leave behind? How do I find meaning in the suffering and loss of friends and others close to me? Are these years that I have ahead of me to be a blessing or a curse?

The Sacred Aging project was an attempt to provide the Reform movement with an outline of programs and resources with which to begin a dialogue with the "new" Jewish older adults who make up, for many congregations, the majority of members. The new multigenerational cohort of older adults represents one of the most exciting and wonderful challenges to confront American Judaism. The times are changing and so are the spiritual and religious needs of a major part of our constituency. There is now the opportunity to build on the development of what some have called a "new American Judaism," a Judaism that is being molded by the baby boomers. Jessica's search for what was "missing" is a search being undertaken by hundreds of thousands of us. The baby boom generation is now poised to enter what some contemporary students of gerontology refer to as life's "third stage." It is a stage of life that holds great promise, the fear of the unknown, and the challenge of creative life choices. How and what we choose will go a long way in shaping the Jewish community of the twenty-first century and the legacy we bequeath to those who come after us.

Acknowledgments ───────────

THERE ARE MANY PEOPLE WHO HAD A HAND IN helping to create this book. My years as a staff member for the Union for Reform Judaism gave me the opportunity to work with hundreds of congregations in North America. First as a regional director and then as the director of URJ's Department of Jewish Family Concerns, I learned from many wonderful individuals. The chairs of my department, Mort Finkelstein, Jean Abarbanel, and Harriet Rosen, were a constant source of support and inspiration. Likewise, I must thank the many members of the department who devoted their time and resources to shaping unique and valuable programs through the years.

This book was born in a conversation with Rabbi Hara Person, who served, at the time, as editor-in-chief of URJ Press. Hara's support was a necessary first step and, when she moved on to head the CCAR Press, Michael Goldberg came forward to be a mainstay and guide in this process. I am deeply appreciative for all of Michael's kindness and encouragement, and also extend my thanks to the other members of the URJ Press staff, including Jessica Katz, Stephen Becker, Michael Silber, Victor Ney, and Jonathan Levine.

A special thanks also to the leadership of the Union for Reform Judaism for their support in developing our programs. In particular, I am grateful to Rabbi Alexander Schindler (z"l), Rabbi Eric Yoffie, Rabbi Len Thal, Rabbi Dan Freelander, and Rabbi Elliot Kleinman. Our program on Sacred Aging, which undergirds the "theology of relationships," was launched under the guidance of co-chairs Linda Wimmer and Dr. Jacquelyn Browne. They were important sources of creativity and dedication. I also wish to express my appreciation to the many people in our congregations who filled out our surveys and who have participated in countless workshops and seminars conducted by the Sacred Aging project. Many of their thoughts and reflections are included in this book.

I have had numerous conversations in the past years with colleagues and friends regarding the ideas in this book. I would like to thank the following who, in their own special ways, have contributed to this effort. I am deeply grateful for your kindness, support, ideas, and suggestions. Thank you to Rabbi Sandy Seltzer, Rabbi Arnold Sher, Sandra Taradash, Michael Freidman, Carole Sterling, Barbara Shuman, Barbara and Mel Kornbluh, Marshall Zolla, Gil and Harriet Rosen, Jean and Jay Abarbanel, Rabbi Bill Cutter, Michele Prince, Rosanne Selfon, Larry and Gail Simon, Steve Burkett and Beth Glenn, David Friedman, Rabbi Phil Bazeley, Rabbi Andrew Rosenkranz, Ellen Jackofsky, Marcia Hochman, Lynn Levy, Dr. Edward Monte, Dr. Dan Gottlieb, and four very special colleagues: Rabbi Edythe Mencher, Rabbi Jon Kendall, Rabbi Larry Kotok, and "Jake."

A special thank you to Jane Travis-Address; and the Rose-Langston family—Jason, Rebecca, Maya, and Elianna. Finally, to our "main man," Alan Address and the Grumbacher family; and Alex, Liz, and "princess" Ayla. May they know only health and peace.

Introduction —————————————————————

OUR TIME
OF TRANSITION

Man is a creature in search of meaning.
ABRAHAM JOSHUA HESCHEL

THE HEBREW LETTERS *BET, KUF,* AND *SHIN* FORM the root of words associated with looking forward, searching, or seeking. This root is at the heart of the word *m'vakshim*: seekers, searchers. It is a word that encompasses where the baby boom generation is at present. We are *m'vakshim*: Aware that time is passing, aware of our own mortality, we are seeking ways to give our lives meaning. In 1993, Professor Wade Clark Roof wrote one of the first overviews of the changes in the religious and spiritual approaches of the baby boom generation. He wrote of the entrance into middle age as a time of potential transition and personal growth. Roof looked at the evolving contexts of the boomers, challenged the notion that boomers are only self-involved (the so-called "me" generation), and stated firmly that "this is a maturing generation of individuals concerned not just with their own inner lives, but with their outer lives. We sense they are reaching out to commit themselves to something of importance, yearning for relationships and connections, longing for more stable anchors for their lives" (Roof 1993, p. 6). Nearly a decade on, with the first wave of the baby boomers now in their sixties, it is clear that Roof's analysis was right on. We are seeking meaning in light of the reality of time. We are searching for a sense of how to infuse our lives with meaning and purpose in an age of almost constant transition.

Like many of my contemporaries, I have begun to seriously think about the next stage of my life. Maybe you too joke with your friends about what you want to be when you grow up. All of a sudden, however, there is less humor and more drama associated with these conversations. I write this as a variety of life changes, large and small, converge. I am in my midsixties and that old Beatles refrain of "Will you still need me . . . when I'm sixty-four?" has taken on new relevance. Along with many of my generation, I find myself in a time of personal, professional, economic, and spiritual transition. Within a year I saw my work environment radically restructured, my daughter become a mother, my son get laid off and finally rehired, the death of my closest friend, and my mother's transition from an assisted-living facility to a skilled nursing facility and eventual death in July 2011. Too many of my friends have begun to experience health issues, and there is a gnawing sense within my soul that time is finite. Not too long ago I sat in an Erev Shabbat service in order to observe the anniversary of my father's death. As my mind became crowded with memories, I found myself unable to conceive of the reality of the passage of time. The same wonder at where the time has gone overwhelmed me when standing under the chuppah at my daughter's wedding, and again recently in the birthing room as she became a mom. No doubt you have had similar moments as the reality of your own aging and the quickening of time become ever more palpable. Has time lost its meaning? Or is it we who now look at it with different eyes? Our parents were right: the older we get, the quicker time seems to pass.

In the spring of 2008, during Shabbat morning services at the Central Conference of American Rabbis convention held at Hebrew Union College–Jewish Institute of Religion in Cincinnati, the rabbinic class of 1972 was called to the bimah for an *aliyah* to honor our classmate, and Judaism's first ordained female rabbi, Rabbi Sally Priesand. Standing there, I suddenly realized that the last time I stood on that sacred space had been thirty-six years before as a twenty-seven-year-old "rookie" rabbi. Where had those years gone? It seemed, as the cliché reminds us, like only yesterday. All of a sudden, I am looking ahead and not quite sure of what is beyond that horizon. We are being told (not promised) that life spans have increased and that, God and health willing, we may expect to live well into our eighties, nineties, and—who knows?—even to one hundred or beyond. Indeed, the Census Bureau is telling us that one of the fastest-growing segments of the population is people over one hundred years of age. The promise of healthy and positive aging is now open before us. Medical technology can give us answers to how that new age can be reached. But where can we turn when we seek the answer to the question "Why?"

The baby boom generation stands poised to enter the "promised land" of older adult life. Our parents have pioneered the concept of healthy aging. They have been the first cohort to significantly push back the boundaries of longevity. How different from our parents' will our own aging be? Blessed with the benefits of medical technology, infused with a social and political consciousness of the now-historic sixties and seventies, we wonder if the baby boomers will, as we age, really be any different than our parents. Try as we might to discount it, the reality of mortality is upon us. We can run, but we can never hide. So, many of us have begun to return to our Jewish roots and traditions in search of some sense of meaning and purpose. What can Judaism teach us about growing older? The book of Ecclesiastes paints a frightening picture of this passage:

> O Youth, enjoy yourself while you are young! Let your heart lead you to enjoyment in the days of your youth. Follow the desires of your heart and the glances of your eyes— but know well that God will call you to account for such things—and banish care from your mind, and pluck sorrow out of your flesh! For youth and black hair are fleeting. So appreciate your vigor in the days of your youth, before those days of sorrow come and those years arrive of which you will say, "I have no pleasure in them"; before sun and light and moon and stars grow dark, and the clouds come back again after the rain. (Ecclesiastes 11:9–12:2)

No one can deny that, for some, aging is a time of sorrow. We all know people who are or have been in that situation. Perhaps that is one reason there is so much emphasis in contemporary media and pop culture on the issue of health. We are told that exercise and proper diet can help us fight against the "days of sorrow" of Ecclesiastes. Indeed, many of our parents have successfully pushed the boundaries of aging to previously unknown limits. As pioneers, their generation was the first to develop communal, political, and social structures that enhanced and embraced aging as a dynamic phase of life. We know many of these people. They are not sitting around, waiting to die. Medical technology and awareness of healthy lifestyles have allowed them to be on their way to elderhostels, cruises, continuing education venues, and, oftentimes back to work, while in many cases dealing with chronic illness and conditions that would have limited the life and mobility of previous generations. They represent the longest-living, healthiest, most mobile, most affluent, and most spiritually engaged cohort of older adults that has ever existed in Jewish history. Health advances have, in addition to lengthening life spans, created new ethical challenges around issues of loss, pain management, caregiving, mental health, and more. This generation has witnessed the tearing down of stereotypes of aging and the rise of older adults as a political and social force. It was this generation, coming of age during and just after World War II, that began the redefinition of work, retirement, family dynamics, and approaches to health. Economic security has made this revolution possible. The success of the postwar Western economy and the accompanying entitlement programs have allowed millions to benefit from the blessings of medical technology, almost doubling life spans in the United States in the twentieth century. Robert Butler, the founder of New York's International Longevity Center, puts this revolution in perspective:

> In the twentieth century we were offered realistic opportunities for health promotion and disease prevention through public health measures, healthy lifestyles, education, rising wealth and workplace regulation, in addition to application of new knowledge, such as understanding hypertension and atherosclerosis. The advent of possible means to

delay aging and *extend* longevity and the growing encouragement of health promotion/disease prevention converge to offer a strategy that could be adapted by individuals and by society in the twenty-first century. (Butler 2008, p. 13)

The baby boom generation now joins our parents' generation in this evolving revolution. Thirty or forty years ago, we may have been locked in generational and culture wars over the great political and social issues of the day, from Vietnam to civil rights, from Watergate to the famous sixties trilogy of sex, drugs, and rock and roll. Now we are bound together with our parents around such issues as entitlements and caregiving. The baby boomers, perhaps the most studied, analyzed, and discussed generation in American history, are beginning to file for Social Security and are heading for Medicare eligibility. We are being told that turning sixty-two or sixty-five need not be an "end" but the beginning of an opportunity to reinvent and re-vision our own lives and selves. We have the opportunity to enter this new "promised land" of longevity and bring the gifts of time and life experience to bear on shaping a future of meaning and purpose. The choice of how we do this rests with us, and that is an awesome responsibility. Our generation is the first to be part of the longevity revolution, both as witnesses and as participants. Given our generation's unique characteristics, we can begin to examine and surmise how to expand on the pioneering accomplishments of our parents' generation.

The blessing of time is a powerful one. When mixed with technology, health, and economic security, you can create a recipe for creativity and change. How do we go about creating a road map that can help us navigate the years ahead? We will spend the majority of our lives without children in the house. We will, God willing, have not years but decades of adult life stretching before us, as an unknown vista, much like the one that greeted Moses as he emerged from crossing the Sea of Reeds and looked ahead to an unknown future. What will we do with this time? How shall we live? How can we begin to make sense of our own mortality and our own reason for being here? The longevity revolution will also impact family dynamics. Indeed it already is creating major ripples and stresses within family systems, especially when it comes to the issue of caregiving. Living longer is presenting the baby boom generation with questions never before considered. Have we saved enough for our later years? Will this new life stage propel us to change our life course and embark on paths of life that, up to now, had been merely the stuff of dreams and fantasy? New options, choices, and challenges await us, as one writer has observed:

> If life suddenly offers a more generous gift of time, how might people decide to spend it? You can imagine tricky periods of transition, as children realize that they have to rethink their assumptions about how long their parents' lives will affect their own—consider the inheritance that never comes, the matriarchal mantle that never gets passed down. The natural sequential phase of old and new generations—the younger cohort's rise, the start of the older's descent—may no longer fall so neatly in sync, creating tension and confusion. More optimistically, there may be second opportunities for reconciliations and resolutions, as families have the boon of extra years, and the wisdom that comes with it, in which to come to terms. The philosophical impact on family dynamics will be profound as parents continue to lean on children long past retirement themselves and people in their

80's learn what it means, at that age, to still be someone's child. (Dominus 2004, pp. 29–30)

In this new age of longevity, the years that lie ahead can be the most profound and meaningful of our lives. Religion, if it is to have any hold on us, must be able to address the questions of meaning that now begin to preoccupy our psyche. We have lived much of life, experienced joys and sadness, challenges and setbacks. For many, the dreams of youth have faded or been put aside. For some, those dreams have been realized. For others, there are still dreams yet to be fulfilled. Most of us are looking forward and trying to understand from where we have come and what we want for our future before our time runs out. Thus, the *why* questions of life, the questions that form the basis for every religion: Why was I born? Why must I die? Why—for what purpose—am I alive? Religion must provide real-life answers to these real-life questions. The answers we find inform how we see ourselves in relation to our families, our community, and our God, and what we wish our legacy to be.

Judaism provides us with a powerful guide with which to navigate our emerging future. As a community, we are living in the midst of an age of personal, social, and religious transition. This transition is creating a new American Judaism, in large part due to the baby boom generation's desire for personal meaning, purpose, and gratification. As baby boomers age, we will seek to create new institutions, re-vision old ones (like the synagogue), and be more open to personal and familial change. The Jewish baby boomer cohort has led the way in this transition, buttressed by a feeling of security within the American experience, a feeling that has provided fertile ground in which the seeds of transition and change have taken root. Rabbi Edward Feinstein writes of this transition when he notes that "the generation of the late twentieth century has experienced a rupture in time. . . . We can no longer look easily to our past, as have generations before us, for lessons of faith, models of Jewish meaning, and an understanding of the collective Jewish project. Nor can we confidently project ourselves into the future. So much of what was taken for granted in earlier times is now open to question" (Feinstein 2007, p. 2). Even so, as we age and we confront the gift and challenge of time, the role and value of personal relationships will become even more powerful. I speak not of acquaintances; rather, of deep, personal, soulful human relationships that help define us as human beings as they create a buffer against our own fear of being alone and our own denial of death. The most powerful and valuable aspect of our lives, as we grow older, is to be found in the relationships that we create and sustain. Relationships make us complete as human beings, and their absence can cause heartache, loneliness, despair, and even death of the soul. Think of your own life, of those moments of meaning that were enriched when they were shared with someone. Think also of that sense of emptiness when you experienced those moments alone, when your first thought was the desire to rush home to tell or call someone special to share with that person what had taken place, only to realize in the same instant that he or she was no longer alive or present to share the moment. Relationships give us the framework to create our own story. They also remind us that truth, meaning, and purpose come not in a belief in and focus on the self, but in something greater than the self. At no time in life are the power and presence of relationships more necessary and important than in our older years. And so, as *m'vakshim,* as seekers of meaning, we must start our search with the fundamental relationship of our existence.

Chapter 1 —————————————

OUR FUNDAMENTAL RELATIONSHIP

So God created human beings in [the divine] image,
creating [them] in the image of God, creating
them male and female. GENESIS 1:27

וַיִּבְרָא אֱלֹהִים אֶת־הָאָדָם בְּצַלְמוֹ בְּצֶלֶם אֱלֹהִים
בָּרָא אֹתוֹ זָכָר וּנְקֵבָה בָּרָא אֹתָם:

Vayivra Elohim et ha-adam b'tzalmo, b'tzelem Elohim
bara oto zachar u'n'keivah bara otam.

J EWISH TRADITION UNDERSTANDS THAT WE EXIST in a fundamental relationship with something outside ourselves. This is important, given the popular impression that the "self" is the center of concern for baby boomers. Of course, this is precisely the point of looking at our own aging, for it is now that we begin to understand that if all we have is just our "self," then we have very little indeed. Perhaps the writers of the Reform movement's 1970s-era prayer book sensed the eventual shift in the baby boom generation's own spirituality when they included this meditation in *Gates of Prayer*:

Through prayer we struggle to experience the Presence of God. Let us be sure that the One we invoke is the Most High, not a god of battles, of state or status or "success"—but the Source of peace and mercy and goodness. For, truly: "The gods we worship write their names on our faces, be sure of that. And we will worship something— have no doubt of that either. We may think that our tribute is paid in secret in the dark recesses of our heart—but it will out. That which dominates our imagination and our thoughts will determine our life and character. Therefore, it behooves us to be careful what we are worshipping, for what we are worshipping, we are becoming." (Stern 1975, p. 240)

As we begin to understand the power and impact of time, we begin to think of how we can matter. Ecclesiastes 1 sets the stage for this when it reminds us that we are, in the end, part of a greater reality. The language of the chapter is familiar to many, and the power of the words rings truer with every passing year.

> *One generation goes, another comes,*
> *But the earth remains the same forever.*
> *The sun rises, and the sun sets—*
> *And glides back to where it rises.*
> *Southward blowing,*
> *Turning northward,*
> *Ever turning blows the wind;*
> *On its rounds the wind returns.*
> *All streams flow into the sea,*
> *Yet the sea is never full;*

To the place [from] which they flow
The streams flow back again.
All such things are wearisome:
No man can ever state them;
The eye never has enough of seeing,
Nor the ear enough of hearing.
Only that shall happen
What has happened,
Only that occur
Which has occurred;
There is nothing new
Beneath the sun!

(Ecclesiastes 1:4–9)

It is often taught that this reflects a type of pessimism or acceptance of fate in life. After all, if all is in vain, then why care? Yet, many of us come to respond to Ecclesiastes with a life that makes a statement attesting to the fact that we have lived. We want to count for something, stand for something, and know that we have contributed to the greater good. How much more true this becomes as we grow older and we come to understand the preciousness of time and the gift that is life. Ecclesiastes presents to us the tension of what some would see as life's emptiness as contrasted with the search for living a life that has some meaning.

Chaim Potok, in his classic *The Chosen,* attempts to put this tension in the form of a dialogue between father and son. Reuven's father gives a passionate and personal response to Ecclesiastes when he says, "Human beings do not live forever . . . we live less than the time it takes to blink an eye, if we measure our lives against eternity. So we may be asked what value is there to a human life? There is so much pain in the world. What does it mean to have to suffer so much if our lives are nothing more than the blink of an eye? I learned a long time ago, that the blink of an eye in itself is nothing. But, the eye that blinks, that is something. The span of life is nothing. But the man who lives that span, he is something. He can fill that tiny span with meaning, so that its quality is immeasurable, though its quantity may be insignificant. A man must fill his life with meaning, meaning is not automatically given to life. It is hard work to fill one's life with meaning" (Potok 1967, p. 217).

In developing a theology of relationships then, we need to start at the first relationship, the relationship that Ecclesiastes alludes to in its way, and Potok does in his. The text that forms the foundation of our discussion is Genesis 1:27, in which we are reminded that we are created "in the image of God." We are part of something greater than ourselves. We do not exist as a mere accident of sperm and egg. We have been created in a sacred manner and for a special purpose that is unique to each of us. As we grow older, as we reflect on our lives and what we have done, we often wonder, What did it all mean? What difference did I make? As we look forward to the years ahead, those questions become even more significant. The desire, perhaps the need, to stand for something, rests within each of us. The Hebrew word that guides our exploration of this desire is *tzelem*. It is a powerful little word that speaks volumes about how we need to see our lives and how we need to establish and nourish relationships. The word *tzelem* is composed of three letters, *tzadi, lamed,* and *mem*; each letter can teach us something about what we can bring to our own lives and our own relationships. The letters can be understood to represent three classic Jewish values that are part of the foundation of our existence. They speak to needs that we all possess, and help guide us as we try to translate our relationship with God into how we deal with our own lives and our relationships with others.

From the first letter, *tzadi*, we learn about the value of *tzelem*, or what it means to be created in the image of God. Judaism teaches that by the mere fact that we exist, we have value, dignity, and worth, because each of us is created with a part of the sacred in us. Each of us has within us the potential to model the sacred in our lives and in the relationships we create. Each of us, no matter what stage of life or condition in which we find ourselves, stands for something of value.

The challenge, as many know, is how to determine what that special aspect of our existence may be. Part of the gift of longevity is the opportunity to discover our own unique, sacred selves—to recognize the value, dignity, and worth in ourselves. The uniqueness of each of us, and the freedom to search for it, is part of the power of Jewish tradition. In one of his many classic passages, Martin Buber writes:

> Every person born into this world represents something new, something that never existed before, something original and unique . . . there has never been anyone like him in the world, for if there had been something like him, there would have been no need for him to be in the world. Every single man is a new thing in the world and is called upon to fulfill his particularity in the world . . . Every man's foremost task is the actualization of his unique, unprecedented and never recurring potentialities, and not the repetition of something that another, and be it even the greatest, has achieved. (Buber 1998, p. 16)

Buber's idea reflects a midrash from the Babylonian Talmud (*Sanhedrin* 38a), which says that, like coins, each of us is minted from a master, yet each of us retains our own uniqueness. We may share the same physical characteristics of all human beings, but each of our souls is unique and within us we have the potential to seek to celebrate and honor that uniqueness: "Thus, the way by which a man can reach God is revealed to him only through the knowledge of his own being, the knowledge of his essential quality and inclination" (Buber 1998, p.18).

Becoming *m'vakshim* is an invitation to fulfill our uniqueness in the world, to realize that we are part of something greater than our own selves, for our selves are finite and mortal. "We must distinguish," writes Abraham Joshua Heschel, "between being human and human being. We are born human beings. What we must acquire is being human. Being human is the essential—the decisive achievement of a human being" (Heschel 1996, p. 374). The idea of *tzelem,* the essential worth of every human being that we derive from the relationship and partnership with God, teaches us that we are responsible for our own lives: "The transcendent dignity of man implies not only inalienable rights but also incredible responsibility" (Heschel 1972, p. 155). Age is no barrier to or excuse from seeking to infuse a sense of justice, dignity, worth, and value into our lives and our relationships. Longevity and changes in family dynamics may add to our responsibilities in the world, but Judaism as a set of responsibilities and duties also implores us to remember that we have responsibilities both to ourselves and to others as we age. Indeed, *tzelem* can remind us of the need to achieve a sense of balance in our lives as we grow older. You cannot respect the worth of yourself and others if you are not living a balanced life that keeps you physically, emotionally, and spiritually healthy.

Indeed, a recipe for a balanced life can be found in our own tradition. Maimonides wrote of the goal of the golden mean: the need to live a life that is in balance between the needs and desires of the mind, the body, and the soul. Rabbi Simcha Bunam of P'shishkha, a Chasidic master, offered another approach to the need to keep one's self in balance. He commented on the phrase "I am but dust and ashes" (Genesis 18:27), saying that we should keep two pieces of paper in our pockets, with two different messages. When we are low and despondent and filled with doubt, we are to take out the paper that says on it that the world was created for my sake (*bishvili nivra ha'olam*). Yet, when we have those moments when we are filled with our own ego and our own self-worth, we need to take out the paper that reminds us that we are nothing but dust and ashes (*anochi afar va'efer*). As we age, we seek to understand our own sense of worth and uniqueness, and we learn that feeling good about our own lives is more powerful and meaningful than accumulating the material "toys" that may have driven us when we were younger. We come to value people and the intimacy that relationships with people can provide for us, which becomes a more important part of our self-definition than any job title or professional role, which, as we come to understand, is transitory.

As we move forward in our lives, we also recognize the need for the value implicit in *tzelem*'s second letter, the *lamed*. *Lamed* is the first letter of the Hebrew word for heart, *lev*. For thousands of years and across many cultures, the heart has been seen as the symbol and source of love, and it is love that is the keystone of the three-value constellation we find in *tzelem*. What is more crucial to cementing and supporting our relationships than love? "We are created in God's image, and we are created in relationship; not fully being an 'I' until there is the other who we can love" (Ochs

1994, p. 7). It is not necessarily romantic love that this *lamed* represents. It is the sense of commitment, intimacy, support, and caring that becomes even more powerful as we age. As we grow older, what means more to us than anything? It is being with someone, being in a relationship with others, and seeking community. Again, think about those moments in your life that have become so precious and meaningful and how much those moments were enhanced by having shared them with someone special. Think also about how so many people are now alone—either psychologically or physically alone—and who, in their souls, crave nothing more than a touch, a caress, a relationship with another human being, a relationship that affirms their existence and helps give texture and definition to life.

For some of us, an increasing awareness of the centrality of relationships stands in stark contrast to the society in which most us were raised. For many, the culture of America put a high priority on individual accomplishments and self-reliance. The price of autonomy may have been the loss of intimacy. In the 1990s, some voices were already warning of this cost. Robert Bellah's *Habits of the Heart* and Robert Putnam's *Bowling Alone* focused on the loss of community. James Jones wrote that the fear of intimacy was related to a fear of losing one's self: "To protect ourself against the pain we have learned to associate with intimacy, we avoid closeness with others and with God. Such connections often remain elusive because they touch our deepest fear and anxiety—born of our false selves—that relationships with others and with a universal and cosmic presence lead to the loss of the individuality and autonomy that we prize so much. These forces within us interfere with our desire for relationships" (Jones 1995, p. 73). Jones goes on to warn against overreliance on technology at the expense of the personal and seems to channel, in a way, the *Gates of Prayer* meditation, on the one hand, and the growth of "virtual" community, on the other, when he writes that "the exaltation of individuality at the expense of relationship and a narrow minded reliance on technical efficiency alone can easily take root in personalities deformed by being raised in an atmosphere of detachment. The worship of autonomy and efficiency provides ready rationalizations for these styles of false selfhood. Raised in an impersonal milieu, the offspring of modernity often lack the psychological resources for authentic intimacy. They are easy prey for the purveyors of counterfeit community" (Jones 1995, p. 88). This tension between autonomy and intimacy with others was also anticipated by Betty Friedan in her classic work from the 1990s, *The Fountain of Age*. She notes the need to risk throwing off the norms of autonomy to embrace relationships. Friedan cites numerous scientific studies that show the power of relationships in fostering health and "vital aging." She argues that we have a unique capacity for caring, intimacy, and love and that we cherish them more as we age and seek increased connectedness. Friedan also sees in our aging and restructuring of life an opportunity to risk the development of new relationships, especially when the patterns of youth and middle age may no longer hold fast. We may be transitioning from full-time work, our children may be scattered, our parents far away as well, or in a state of gradual decline. Friends become ever so much more important, relationships so much more powerful: "Some more organic or intensive way must be found to sustain real intimacy. Our 'given' bonds—of family, school, profession, marriage, children, grandchildren—are no longer automatically renewed. And new bonds are no longer automatically given as we move into late life. It is all a matter of choice now. That's scary, but it's also liberating, if we are strong enough to admit our need for that intimacy, and keep on risking—pain, rejection, the unknown—to find new ways of creating these intimate bonds" (Friedan 1993, p. 292). The most powerful aspect of *tzelem* is our need for love, for intimacy, and for caring and being cared for. Love is the force that propels us to move beyond our self and into a dialogue with the world. Love is the innate need that we all possess to combat the fear of being alone.

Genesis 2:18 is the key verse that underscores this need for love. In it we read that it is not good for us to be *l'vado*, alone. It is almost as if Genesis is aware of the tensions that can be illustrated by these two words beginning with *lamed*, *lev* (heart) and *l'vado* (alone). This is a powerful word, *l'vado*. We have all been there. We have all had moments in life when we have felt "alone." We could be in the middle of a stadium throng, a crowded street or airplane; and we have felt cut off, isolated, and lost. Psychotherapist Irvin D. Yalom offers an interesting interpretation of *l'vado* in seeing two types of loneliness: everyday and existential. The everyday or "interpersonal" type of loneliness refers to a feeling of being "isolated" from others, of feeling unloved or incapable of intimacy. Yalom's existential loneliness is more profound. This he identifies as a gap between people: "This gap is a consequence not only of each of us having been thrown alone into existence and having to exit alone, but derives from the fact that each of us inhabits a world fully known only to ourselves" (Yalom 2008, pp. 120–121). Genesis understands that this condition is harmful, that it causes illness and fear. Marc Gafni explains:

> The original Hebrew word for "alone" is *l'vado*. When God uses it in the creation story, it can be rendered most accu-

rately not as being physically alone but as "lonely." God is essentially saying to us, "It is not good for the human being to be lonely." As long as the human being is lonely, all the good of creation cannot sate him. . . . As long as the human being feels alienated, separate from, and empty, then all the objective goods of the universe will be irrelevant. That is the experience of loneliness—to feel apart from, severed from, alienated and empty. (Gafni 2001, p. 9)

Reflect for a moment on these interpretations of *l'vado*. It is not good that we exist *l'vado*, cut off, isolated, withdrawn from our world and our own unique self. Yet each of us, as we grow older, often looks back on our journey and reflects on those moments when we felt alone, as if we were wandering in our own wilderness, seeking community, searching for love. In light of this understanding of *l'vado* and our own sociocultural reality, we can see a deeply powerful symbol of our own search for meaning in the Passover story. I believe that every one of us is represented by the Passover story. How many of us struggle to free ourselves from some sort of "slavery"? It could be a job that binds us or a relationship that is stagnant. It could be the dream to do something that we have always wished to do but have never had the time or courage to pursue. How many of us, like Moses, feel lost in some wilderness, searching for guidance and a sense of our own redefined Torah? How many of us have sat around the seder table, looking at the generations and feeling both joy in those present and a sense of aloneness thinking of those no longer with us or of what might have been in our own journey. We are, each of us, the Four Children in the Haggadah, always asking "Why?" What is that story other than a metaphor for own personal journeys from exile to redemption; from *l'vado* to *lev*; a longing for community, a dream of having a loving relationship and a wish for a sense of life's wholeness?

The journey from *l'vado* to *lev* reflects studies on mental health issues that focus on the stresses and strains associated with midlife. For it is then that we become reacquainted with a different type of exile that may be having an impact on us—an exile of our soul from a sense of meaning as life quickens and our own mortality hovers. *L'vado*, then, is a form of real and present exile. It inhibits that sense of uniqueness and value, worth and justice that comes from the idea of *tzelem*. It is so strong that it propels us to seek connection and, we pray, a sacred connection; for the opposite creates danger and self-destruction: "The primal drive that propels us in Biblical consciousness is the drive to move from loneliness to loving, from separation to union, from the pain of rupture to the rapture of connection" (Gafni 2001, p. 8). The idea of *lev* builds on the foundation of *tzelem*. The desire for connection, intimacy, and relationship is a means by which we can validate our unique selves. Without it, we are in exile. In attempting to describe our need for connection, Rav Joseph B. Soloveitchik, in his classic *The Lonely Man of Faith*, expressed it this way: our "quest is for a new kind of fellowship, which one finds in the existential community. There, not only hands are joined, but experiences as well; there, one hears not only the rhythmic sound of the production line, but also the rhythmic beat of hearts starved for existential companionship and all embracing sympathy and experiencing the grandeur of the faith commitment; there, one lonely soul finds another soul tormented by loneliness and solitude yet unqualifiedly committed" (Soloveitchik 1965, p. 40). There is much to this *lev-l'vado* tension. Baby boomers have been raised in the American culture of personal autonomy, individuality, and self-reliance. Will this change as we ourselves age? Are we beginning to realize that without a sense of community, without intimacy and connection with others, our lives, despite any economic and social success, may remain *l'vado*? Are we so afraid of intimacy and closeness that we create barriers to them?

Lev reminds us that at the "heart" of the concept of *tzelem* is the need for love, connection, and relationships. Like our fundamental relationship with God, love transcends the physical world. Love is the mortar that holds memory in our souls. Think again of all those special people in your life who may not be with you now. Some have moved, some you have lost touch with, and others have died. Memory keeps them in our mind and soul, and love cements those memories and propels us to remember all that is good in our lives. We live in a world that too often ignores the power of love and relationships. We live in a world that too often has made love a commodity, a slogan, or a commercialized, exploited ideal. Yet as we march on in our own life journeys, what is the emotion that stirs us and continues to give our lives meaning, hope, desire, and direction? It is love. It is the need, basic and primal, to be in relationship with another human being: "More and more psychologists have found that for older persons, loneliness is not necessarily linked to the death of a spouse or to how infrequently they see their children and grandchildren, but to the *absence of personal relationships with peers*, friends of their own age or any age who share their interests and with whom they sustain their roots of shared experience" (Friedan 1993, p. 385). When we have these connections, we feel part of something greater than our own self. We have a sense of partnership, shared purpose, connection, and peace. When we lack these connections, we are adrift, alone, in exile, *l'vado*. And in the face of the ultimate aloneness of our own death, nothing is more powerful than the embrace of love, for it is that love that forms the heart of Judaism's concept of eternal life.

The uniqueness of our own life journey and the need to embrace that journey and infuse it with love lead us to *tzelem*'s third letter, *mem*. The value that this letter represents is mitzvah. Mitzvot, the sacred obligations of our tradition, are there to propel us into the world. Our uniqueness can be measured in relationship to others. Our involvement with the world at large, with other people, can give us the means by which we negotiate our own need for love and community, allowing us to stand fast against a sense of isolation, personal exile, and aloneness. Mitzvot, the means by which we engage and strengthen our relationship with God, self, and community, are the meaning-seeking acts that bridge our relationship between ourselves and God and ourselves and the community. Mitzvot are actions, and it is in the doing, in being involved with others, in creating relationships that we translate and model the values inherent in *tzedek* and *lev*. This speaks to the basic Jewish belief that we cannot be Jewish by ourselves. To be fully engaged in the Jewish world we need to seek out community, establish relationships, engage others; for in doing so we come to see more of our own soul and self. This mandate pervades Jewish history and experience. The tradition requires a community of ten people for prayer. Our festivals and celebrations are enhanced and defined by being shared with family and friends. The recitation of sins on Yom Kippur is recited in community and uses the plural form of the Hebrew. Our literature implores us to always be at the ready to do the mitzvah and to not separate ourselves from the bonds of community. Indeed, it is via the mitzvah that we bring the sense of *tzelem* into the world. We build community by becoming the active presence of God in the world. We build relationships by our involvement with others. We do not build community and establish relationships by being passive or by withdrawing into a self-imposed world of isolation and asceticism. We find our "self" in service, for the mitzvah is the steel that reinforces the structure of community. That is why so many synagogues, realizing that their patterns of affiliation are changing and that a sense of community is waning, have pursued so strongly the creation of "inreach" programs of what is called "caring community." Slowly, there is a developing recognition and understanding among many synagogue leaders that the primary means for the establishment and continuity of community is not an emphasis on programming, but a renewed dedication to creating sacred relationships within that community. Much of the spiritual revolution of contemporary North American Judaism is being driven by baby boomers who, having been members of congregations, now demand that these congregations be present for the life issues that they are facing in the early twenty-first century: caregiving, children leaving home, health and wellness, and the need to make sense out of what we hope will be decades of life to come. When these needs are not met, we see the rise of niche communities: small group enclaves, much like the *chavurah* models of a few decades ago, that cater and respond to the need for an intimate, personal communal experience. We are also witnessing the rise of alternative minyanim that often emerge from congregational members who, while keeping a nominal affiliation, seek a smaller, more intimate worship experience. One such group in Pittsburgh draws a small cadre of people who share a love of informal worship and study and who meet monthly for Friday night Erev Shabbat dinner in one of the group members' homes, filling the evening with music and study. Joan and Jerry, a sixtyish couple from suburban Philadelphia, explained to me at a dinner and discussion on the changing nature of boomer affiliation that they much prefer to engage in a smaller gathering of friends who share their experiences. I asked why they still paid dues to belong to their congregation when they freely admitted that they received so little from it. They responded that they did it because many of their friends were still members and it made it easier on the High Holy Days, when their children came in from out of town, to be able to go as a family to services. Yet they rarely attended events and services during the rest of the year, as those moments were geared, they concluded, to constituencies whose needs did not reflect what was going on in their lives. They were facing issues of their own illnesses, the "letting go" of children, and their own transitions, as well as still caring for a parent. They felt a need for connection, affirmation of their life challenges, and a yearning for a community of meaning. The search for a community of meaning is, I think, one of *the* great drives of contemporary life. Over lunch at a Philadelphia deli, David, an old high school friend, explained that he realized the centrality and healing power of relationships as he battled cancer. Like so many of those with whom we spoke and who responded to our survey in the Sacred Aging project, the overwhelming source of those supporting relationships came from a cadre of friends and family. David regretted that his former synagogue was unable to provide the sense of caring support that he needed. To not respond to these concerns in a caring and supportive way is to court irrelevance. That is a major choice now emerging within our synagogue world. It is why emphasizing community and connection has never been more vital.

We derive a sense of our own uniqueness and gifts by the mitzvah of involvement with others, by serving with others. Being present with people builds relationships, and relationships enhance our own quality of life. Rachel Naomi Remen writes that the powerful call to find oneself through service with others is a response to the fear of being alone and of our own mortality:

> All who serve, serve life. What we serve is something worthy of our attention, of the commitment of our time and our lives. Service is not about fixing life, outwitting life, manipulating life, controlling life, or struggling to gain mastery over life. When we serve, we discover that life is holy. Service is closer to generosity than it is to duty. It connects us to one another and to life itself. When we experience our connectedness, serving others becomes the natural and joyful thing to do. Over the long run, fixing and helping are draining but service is renewing. When you serve, your work will sustain you, renew you, and bless you, often over many years. The best definition of service I have come across is a single word. Belonging. Service is the final healing of isolation and loneliness, it is the lived experience of belonging. (Remen 2000, pp. 199–200)

We are already seeing that baby boomers are redefining their sense of growing older and are not shy about changing traditional definitions of work, social activism, and community organization. These are all aspects of honoring the concept of mitzvah, to continue to seek meaning through relationships and connections through causes, so that we may continue to define our uniqueness in life. Likewise, it is through the action of being in the world, of doing mitzvot, that we actualize our being in God's image and likeness.

> The Bible speaks of man as having been created in the likeness of God, establishing the principle of *an analogy of being*. In his very being, man has something in common with God. Beyond the analogy of being, the Bible teaches the principle of an *analogy in acts*. Many may act in the likeness of God. It is in this likeness of acts—"to walk in His ways"—that is the link by which man may come close to God. To live in such likeness is the essence of imitation of the Divine. (Heschel 1955, p. 289)

We honor the people and the possibilities of those who have and may, thanks to our involvement with them, create good in society. This idea of an active, mitzvah-oriented life is, as we shall see in the next chapter, a way in which we can define our own sense of meaning and purpose in the world.

Tzadi, *lamed*, and *mem*—uniqueness, love, and deed—create a foundation on which we can build a life of meaning and purpose as we enter the revolutionary time of life that now awaits us. Being a *tzelem* is not passive. As *m'vakshim*, as seekers of meaning, we are being called to see *tzelem* not as a noun, but as a verb. A Jewish response to the reality of the aging revolution is to see our lives as a vehicle through which *tzelem Elohim* is seen and understood as a validation of the need for our continuing involvement in life, in our continuing growth as human beings, and as a guilt-free permission not to dwell on the past but to use our experience and the lessons of our lives to create a sacred future. On this foundation of *tzelem*, we create relationships that help define our uniqueness, embrace us with love and intimacy, and give us the support we need to bring our message of meaning into the world: "We seek out relationships because we need other people in our lives. Our actions are the foundations of those relationships, and only through Torah's insistence on mutual respect will those bonds be sustained" (Twerski 2009, p. 41). Judaism embraces life, no matter at what stage in that journey we may find ourselves. We have been created for a sacred purpose. But what, we often wonder, is that purpose? We, who are now moving into the autumn of our lives, search for our own sense of meaning and purpose. At times, is seems as if the questions we have outweigh the possible answers. In that, we may not be different from our tradition, for the Torah begins with a question that speaks to our own search. It is, perhaps, *the* question that we spend our lives trying to answer. It is God's question to us, drawn from the innocence and bliss of the idealized Eden.

Chapter 2 ———————————————————

THE FUNDAMENTAL QUESTION

But God Eternal called out to the man, saying,
"Where are you?" Genesis 3:9

וַיִּקְרָא יְהֹוָה אֱלֹהִים אֶל־הָאָדָם וַיֹּאמֶר לוֹ אַיֶּכָּה׃

Vayikra Adonai Elohim el ha-adam vayomer lo, ayecka?

I N Genesis 3, we confront the most powerful and meaningful question in the Torah. It is, I believe, the default question raised by Jewish tradition, and it is the question we spend our lives trying to answer: *Ayecha?* Where are you? In the book of Genesis, it is asked by God of Adam and Eve as they hide in the Garden of Eden. It is asked of us by God at many times in our lives, but with increasing frequency as we age. What does it mean to ask, *Ayecha?* Who am I? Why am I here? What purpose does my life serve?

The wonderful and powerful Eden story is one of the most important chapters of Torah, for it introduces us to the one reality from which we cannot escape: our own death. The Eden story is an attempt by the biblical author to reconcile this final reality with the "good" and perfect world of God's creation. The solution is set up in Genesis 3, in the dialogue between Eve and the serpent, when Eve, responding to the serpent's taunts, says, "We may eat of the fruit of the other trees in the garden, it is only about the fruit of the tree in the middle of the garden that God said: You shall not eat of it or touch it, lest you die" (Genesis 3:2–3). Of course, the serpent goads Eve by saying, "You are not going to die" (Genesis 3:4), as if to reinforce the fantasy that we somehow can evade the finality of our own death. And indeed Adam and Eve do not die in this chapter. Rather, the awareness of our own mortality is represented by the admission that Adam and Eve become "afraid." God asks, "Where are you?" and Adam answers, "I heard the sound of You in the garden, and I was afraid, because I was naked" (Genesis 3:10). What was their fear? All of a sudden, they had become aware of their unique "human" situation. This awareness transforms their reality. The "naked" reality of our own eventual death is what we come to "know." We may try to deny this reality, repress it, or fight it; yet, it is our future.

In the Eden story, then, Adam and Eve learn to fear death, and hide from it. But God will not shield them from this knowledge. God comes looking for them. In asking *Ayecha?* God is not simply asking where Adam and Eve are hiding, but where they are in their understanding of their own mortality. As we grow older, we become more aware of the short span of our life. We feel it mostly on an unconscious level, surfacing sometimes when we are confronted by a friend's or family member's illness or death. *Ayecha*, however, is not a call to fear death; rather, it is a call to wake up and celebrate life. God's *ayecha* is present and becomes more powerful as we age. In her book on Genesis, Avivah Zornberg suggests that *ayecha* is really an invitation. Citing the commentator Rashi, she sees "Where are you?—as an invitation to response, to dialogue. In confrontation with God, Adam's salvation can only lie in creating his own reality" (Zornberg 1995, pp. 117–18). *Ayecha* calls on us to enter into sacred dialogue with God and with the journeys our lives have taken and will take in the future. It is a dialogue that, hopefully, pushes us to seek our own sense of uniqueness, our own truth. It is through this dialogue that we can begin to see our own mortality and what our legacy can be for those who come after us.

In his book *Spirituality and Aging*, Robert Atchley, one of the leading scholars on aging and the role of the spirit, notes that our interest in spiritual development as we age is prompted by questions such as "Is this all there is? What does it all mean? How do I fit into the picture? What will happen to me when I die? How can I leave a legacy for future generations? How can I give back to a world that has nurtured me? Do I need to get even with a world that hasn't nurtured me? These and many other questions fuel a spiritual journey that for most people becomes more intentional in midlife" (Atchley 2009, p. 113). We are becoming more aware of our own selves, not in an egotistical way, but in a spiritual way, and, to paraphrase the therapist Irvin Yalom, that growing self-awareness results from our increasing awareness of the "wound of mortality." As Yalom points out, "Our existence is forever shadowed by the knowledge that we will grow, blossom, and inevitably, diminish and die . . . Death is destiny. Your wish to survive and your dread of annihilation will always be there. It's instinctive—built into your protoplasm—and has a momentous effect on how you live" (Yalom 2008, pp. 1, 115). Yalom cites this "death anxiety" as the "mother of all religions, which, in one way or another attempt to temper the anguish of our finitude" (Yalom 2008, p. 5).

Can religion then be seen as a way in which humankind has sought to deal with the inevitability of death? This very important and powerful question reminds me of a class that I took many years ago as a third-year rabbinic student at the Hebrew Union College in Cincinnati. Dr. Alvin Reines (z"l) gave an elective on the history of Reform Judaism. Dr. Reines was a professor of philosophy and keeper of the major "flunk" course in the third year, a course on Maimonides. It was the one class that, if you managed to pass it, meant another major barrier to ordination had been overcome. The elective was given on a Wednesday afternoon, in the library. It was an exploration of the philosophy of Reform Judaism and of religion in general. It was also one of those classes that remain with you because of one lecture. That lecture was at the opening of the semester when we started to discuss the *why* of religion. We began by looking at Genesis 3 and discussing what undergirded the story. We looked at some of the pre-Hebrew mythologies, like Gilgamesh, and eventually were led to the role of our own finitude. Dr. Reines then gave us the theory that religion began when humankind's desire to live forever came into direct conflict with the reality that we will all die. That frenetic confrontation resulted in the birth of religion. Or, in terms of Genesis 3, it resulted in humankind's call to answer *ayecha*.

God walks the garden in search of God's creations. They hide and deflect responsibility, as we often do. God is in search of us as we, in our way, are in search of God. Abraham Joshua Heschel is one of our great teachers on this story, noting the symbiotic relationship that exists between God and us. God asked then, and continues to ask now: *Ayecha*—Where are you? We spend our lives trying to answer that one question. We develop different answers at different times in our lives. As we gaze at what we hope will be years of life before us, we come to ask ourselves, Where are we now? What is it that I wish to do for the rest of my life? In his book

Who Is Man? Heschel puts these question to us from a context that sees the search for meaning as something greater than just a drive for personal contentment. He raises the level of discussion of what we want for the rest of our lives from the mundane and temporal to the spiritual and transcendent.

> What I look for is not to gain a firm hold on myself and on life, but primarily how to live a life that would deserve and evoke an eternal Amen. It is not simply a search for certitude (though that is implied in it) but for personal relevance, for a degree of compatibility; not an anchor of being, but a direction of being. It is not enough for me to be able to say "I am"; I want to know *who I am,* and in relation to whom I live. It is not enough for me to ask questions; I want to know how to answer the one question that seems to encompass everything I face: What am I here for? (Heschel 1965, pp. 52–53)

Why was I born? Why am I here? Why must I die? These are the questions that flow from God's *ayecha,* questions that grow in importance as we grow older and attain a deeper sense of our own mortality. To be able to truly answer God's *ayecha,* we must first "know" or be aware of our own unique humanity and the reality of our own mortality. The most precious way that we can find meaning in the face of death is through our relationships with other people and in the creation of communities. I do not think it is a coincidence that the warning not to eat from the tree of knowledge (Genesis 2:17) comes immediately before the verse that reminds us that it is not good to be *l'vado,* alone (Genesis 2:18). As we become more aware of our own mortality, our need for people and connection grows. That is why so many of us fear a protracted illness or old age that is confined to a "facility" in which we may be cut off from friends, family, or community. Or, as is happening with some of our parents' generation, we fear outliving spouses, friends, community, finances, and even, God forbid, children—and doing so alone. In the face of the ultimate aloneness, we want to mean something. We do not wish to see ourselves as an accident of nature, but as a purposeful creation. We are "creatures in search of meaning":

> The pursuit of meaning is meaningless unless there is meaning in pursuit of man. To the Biblical mind, man is not only a creature who is constantly in search of himself, but also a creature God is constantly in search of. Man is a creature in search of meaning because there is meaning in search of him, because there is God's beseeching question, "Where art Thou?" (Heschel 1972, p. 163)

Ayecha means there is a purpose for us, seeking us, searching for us. This is not some New Age "find your bliss" search; rather, it is something that is at the heart of our tradition. Each of us has a purpose for being alive. Each of has a reason, a meaning that is searching for us, just as we are searching for it.

Rob, in responding to one of the surveys on attitudes about aging, wrote, "I am looking for more meaning in my relationship with Judaism as I feel less meaning in my professional and personal pursuits." It is no coincidence that so much of the revolution in Jewish learning and spirituality is being led by people like Rob. Many of us are transitioning from one type of work to another. Sometimes this transition is voluntary. Sadly, however, too many have had this transition thrust upon them recently. Yet it has become a time of reevaluation, searching, and, for some, reinvention. It has become a time to explore new possibilities for ourselves, to dig into the well of our own life experience, and, in so doing, to recognize that to seek meaning for nothing but our own self-satisfaction is selfish and negates the power of being in relationship with others. We need to find our sense of meaning in the context of community.

Hillel's eternal question—"If I am only for myself, what am I?" (*Pirkei Avot* 1:14)—is especially relevant in our contemporary world, where so much is focused on the individual and the self. A recurring theme in the Sacred Aging surveys is that people continue to find a sense of meaning and purpose in their relationships. Relationships are the antidote to *l'vado*; they are the means through which we moderate the "death anxiety" and are key to creating communities of caring and support. It is in relationships that we begin to find how to answer *ayecha*. Part of this need for relationships is evidenced in the many members of the baby boom generation looking to "give back" to the community at large. Many boomers were raised with a spirit of activism and involvement. People are searching for a way to bring their passions and interest to bear on society for the greater good. Jeff, in responding to a question on what insights he would want to share as a result of his own life experiences, said: "the importance of sharing, giving back to the Jewish community in terms of time and energy and living a spiritually fulfilled life."

This presents a unique challenge for many congregations and Jewish institutions that are facing this age of transition. The longevity revolution has produced generations of active, involved individuals whose life experience is an untapped resource. This "spiritual capital" represents one of the most powerful consequences of the current boom in aging. The amount of life experience that is not being used to teach, mentor, create, and support other members of a community is a major challenge to us all. The boomer generation's desire to be involved and to give back will benefit those institutions that reach out and embrace the power of their experiences and seek to make use of the gifts of those experiences.

A 2008 study by the Association of Jewish Family and Children's Agencies assessed how the organization's member institutions could harness the resources of the emerging baby boom generation, knowing that this cohort will approach volunteer work differently than did the generation of its parents. The findings supported the idea that there exists within the boomer generation a huge possibility to engage this spiritual capital and that the boomers indicated a strong desire to "give back" to the community and society. The study noted, "Our effectiveness in engaging these extraordinary generations of Americans—meeting them where they are, sensitive to their motivations and barriers, and pulling institutional levers to encourage them to give more—will make a difference in whether our country fulfills its civic promise" (Association of Jewish Family and Children's Agencies 2008, p. 3).

This spirit of giving back has been noted repeatedly in recent years. The idea of "civic engagement," brought to public consciousness by Marc Freedman, has gradually been making its way into increasing numbers of organizations. Dick Goldberg heads one such entity in Philadelphia. Dick directs Coming of Age, which is housed at the Temple University Center for Intergenerational Learning. Dick's work has taken him around the United States working with groups of boomers. He sees the desire to "connect and contribute" to the greater good as endemic to all people. The boomers have a special opportunity to raise this facet of life to a higher level. He maintains that because the boomers prize their autonomy, they want "to tailor their volunteerism to their own schedule," adding that they "would prefer to work in teams, in a collaborative way" (*Focus on Faith*, WNJC-AM 2009). As boomers age, we have a strong desire to do something, but at the same time, to do so on our own terms.

The Berman Jewish Policy Archive's study noted this in terms of a hope that boomers will find satisfaction in giving back to the Jewish community. The study cited one Jewish professional who stated that "baby boomers look for value and meaning differently from their parents. They find meaning beyond the Jewish community, can go where they want, when they want. Those who can be involved seem to get more status outside the Jewish community. This change is serious" (Berman Jewish Policy Archive 2009, p. 6).

How to make meaningful use of a congregation's spiritual capital will be one of the challenges of the next several decades. Dr. Thomas R. Cole and Rabbi Dayle A. Friedman have written about the need to see, in our emerging elder population, a huge reservoir for responsibility. "What should be added," writes Cole, "to revitalize religious understanding of older people as moral agents?" (Cole 2011, p. 158). This turns the conversation about aging from a discussion about what society can do for me to one about my responsibility, as an elder, to leave the world a better place. It includes an ongoing spiritual dialogue among society and self and God, much as Moses had with God and the Children of Israel, as Friedman writes (Friedman 2011, p. 160). Aging as a stage of moral responsibility can be a powerful approach to seeking, as *m'vakshim*, our own response to God's *ayecha*.

The acceptance of the reality of mortality, the fact that we are the only creatures aware of our own finitude, is reflected in a wonderful formula in *Pirkei Avot* 3:1. The text is written in the name of the first-century sage Akavya ben Machalelel, who states: "Concentrate on three things and you will not fall into the grip of sin. Know from where you came, where you are going, and before Whom you will have to give account and reckoning." Reuven Bulka, in his commentary on this passage, asserts that Akavya may be addressing someone who, like many of us, is awakening to the richness and potential meaning of our lives. "Akavya," according to Bulka, "says the starting point is to recognize that one's roots and one's destination, physically, are of insignificance; that the only significance that can be lent to life is in the period between the beginning and the end" (Bulka 1993, p. 96). Bulka goes on to assert that Akavya's words point to "ultimate values; values which transcend even death itself and which give a meaning to life beyond the physical" (Bulka 1993, p. 96). Judaism's emphasis on living life in the "now" speaks to this, and we will encounter this belief again in our discussion of Deuteronomy 30. In trying to answer God's *ayecha*, we are taught to start in the here and now. The tradition reminds us that, although we are the product of what has come before us, we cannot control what that past was, and it may be folly to try to manipulate what will be. So we start in the here and now to find out where we might be going and, as we shall explore, how Judaism empowers us to change the direction of our lives as we seek to discover our own uniqueness.

The gift of time and longevity is the opportunity to create moments and lives of meaning. It is a gift that calls on us to forge our own theology of meaning, a theology that springs from the lessons we have learned from our own experiences and based on the relationships that we have created and that help sustain us. Time is a gift that we do not control and whose value and importance grows as we age. Randy Pausch, a college professor who wrote his reflections on time as he was dying, put it simply: "Time is all you have. And you may find out one day that you have less than you think" (Pausch 2008, p. 111). It is this search for our own unique self that will allow us to develop our own responses to the eternal *ayecha* and to find our sense of meaning within the community at large. This is now our time to seriously seek answers to the *why* questions of Genesis 3. These are the basic questions of life, the questions at the root of religion. They are not theoretical or abstract. They are the questions that gnaw at us in the quiet moments of our lives, in the dark recesses of our souls that we often fear to visit for we are too afraid to find the answers. They are the questions whose importance is now heightened as the reality of our own mortality becomes apparent. They are the questions that call to us, as did God's voice in Eden, and for which we need to find the courage to go forth and seek the answers.

LETTING GO AND MOVING FORWARD

The Eternal One said to Abram, "Go forth from your land,
your birthplace, your father's house, to the land that I will
show you.   GENESIS 12:1

וַיֹּאמֶר יְהוָה אֶל־אַבְרָם לֶךְ־לְךָ מֵאַרְצְךָ וּמִמּוֹלַדְתְּךָ
וּמִבֵּית אָבִיךָ אֶל־הָאָרֶץ אֲשֶׁר אַרְאֶךָּ:

Vayomer Adonai el Avram, lech l'cha mei-artzcha u-mimolad't'cha
u-mibeit avicha el ha-aretz asher arecha.

———————

Now Jacob was left alone, and a man wrestled with him
until the rise of dawn.   GENESIS 32:25

וַיִּוָּתֵר יַעֲקֹב לְבַדּוֹ וַיֵּאָבֵק אִישׁ עִמּוֹ עַד עֲלוֹת
הַשָּׁחַר:

Vayivateir Yaakov l'vado vayeiaveik ish imo ad alot hashachar.

J AY CARSEY HAD EVERYTHING. HE LIVED THE PER-
fect life in the perfect suburb. He lived well, was well
respected, and, to anyone looking in, seemed to "have it
all." Then one day, he left his perfect home, drove to the airport,
boarded an airplane, and disappeared. Jay is the main figure in a

43

disturbing book titled *Exit the Rainmaker*. He stands for so many of us who one day look around, assess the passing of time and our place in that passage, and ask, "Is this it?" We can never really determine when these questions of meaning will surface. As we baby boomers transition into our own aging, these questions take on a new importance, a new sense of urgency. The AARP's Harry (Rick) Moody, Ph.D., a well-known expert on aging, places this gnawing sense of unease in a spiritual context, in that "little voice" that we all have somewhere in our own souls, the little voice that at times goads us, warns us, pushes us, and brings us up short. It is always there and usually appears when we least expect it or want to hear it. It is the voice that appears to us to remind us that the clock of our life span is ticking with increasing rapidity, that we are not as young as we used to be. "Is this all there is? it asks. This home? This mate? This job? This life? Time is running out, it whispers . . . There is one thing we do know for sure, however: this little voice has a way of provoking rebellious thoughts. Wasn't life supposed to get better and better as the years pass? we ask. Didn't I do what I was supposed to do: go to school, join the team, work hard, pay my dues?" (Moody 1997, p. 4).

Sooner or later we all come to the place in our lives when we confront that disturbing, uncomfortable, and yet powerful question that God keeps asking: *Ayecha*—Where are you, where am I? Living life as an active response to *ayecha* requires us to give ourselves permission to grow and evolve. That growth may require taking risks, and it will always involve the acceptance and embrace of change. The re-visioning of work, retirement, and relationships that we are witnessing with the aging of the baby boomers indicates that we will be, all things being equal, a generation that will continue to seek out new ways of growth, change, and personal evolution. A Jewish approach to aging is one that celebrates this change and growth. This is one of our great challenges, for it seems that as we age, we are too easily able to find reasons not to keep looking forward. Too often we accept a life that falls short of one that fully engages our potential. Too often the reasons are all valid, each in their own way; yet if we lose our ability to reinvent our selves, if we quietly accept things as they are and lose our capacity for dreaming and visioning, we run the risk of a slow death of the spirit. We court the danger of being cut off from the mystery of our own life's potential. Two episodes in Genesis help give clarity to the challenge of moving forward versus staying put. Both episodes can be read as metaphors for our own life's journey. Both episodes involve the courage to risk, the challenges of living with change, and the faith to seek a new understanding of life's meaning.

Abraham, in Genesis 12, is told by God to go forth from his native land to the "land that I will show you." He uproots his family and leaves behind the only life he has known to "go forth." Like many of us, Abraham's dramatic change takes place only after a major life event. Abraham is "freed" to go forth after his father's death, enabling him to move forward. How many of us have been like Abraham, tied to a place, a circumstance for very good reasons? And then, the circumstances change and the possibilities present themselves to move forward. How many of us have done so? How many of us have been an Abraham and said yes to the future, even when we did not know the land into which we were going? How many of us, how many of the people we know, found reasons not to go? How many have stayed, fearing the unknown or rationalizing that they have grown comfortable or are now "too old to change"? The text from Genesis shows that Judaism is accepting and encouraging of our ability to move forward into places we do not know. Indeed, at times we may have to in order to survive, either in a physical sense or in an emotional or spiritual sense. It is part of the embrace of life's mystery. It is part of our response to God's *ayecha*. It is also fraught with fear. It is, as we know, comfortable to maintain the status quo. We play the never-ending game of "What if . . . ?" and envision catastrophic fantasies of all the things that could go wrong if we were to opt for change.

Abraham is not a wild-eyed youth who sets off on a coming-of-age journey. He is a mature family man who carries the weight of many responsibilities. We can almost imagine him caring for his aging father, content to make the best of things, which are, in truth, not so bad after all. Yet, after his father's death, it is as if he understands that God's call is really his soul calling to seek the meaning in his life that must be found. The time is at hand and to refuse would be to settle. How many of us have conversed with God in similar situations? Arguing back and forth, feeling the push-pull of "Should I stay or should I go?" Life is too short to live in exile from our true self. Abraham heeds the call:

> Abraham's advanced age is what makes his leap of faith so impressive. His mid-life crisis is a familiar phenomenon, but his response to it is not. Most of us gripe about our lives and fantasize about making a radical change. But how many among us actually heed our soul's call to "go forth"? Most of us conclude we are better off bearing whatever disappointments we may harbor in our lives. By the time we reach middle age we have too much at stake to make bold course corrections. We have our reputations to worry about, assets to protect, bills to pay, children to feed and educate and parents to care for. Rather than take a blind

leap into the unknown, we usually settle for buying a new car or taking up a new hobby. Abraham remains an inspirational model because he demonstrates the power of faith to overcome cynicism, despair and defeatism at any age. (Rosenblatt 1995, p. 105)

Why should age be a barrier to change? We have moved forward all our lives. From the time we emerged from the womb, our lives have been about moving forward and changing. Growth is part of life and, as I think our tradition tells us, is not bound by the number of years we have lived. Not moving forward implies the real danger of getting stuck in a life situation that freezes us. "The Bible tells us that as she looked back on the destruction of Sodom and Gomorrah, Lot's wife was turned into a pillar of salt. I suspect that many of us have had this happen to us without our realizing we have become frozen, trapped by the past. We are holding on to something long gone, and hands full, are unable to take hold of our opportunities on what life is offering" (Remen 1995, p. 195). Failure to move forward, to change, courts a spiritual death of the soul that can render anyone lifeless.

The Midrash (*B'midbar Rabbah* 13:7) tells us that as the Children of Israel stood poised to enter the Sea of Reeds, and thus their future, they were paralyzed with fear and indecision. To "go forth" meant taking a huge risk, based on faith in an uncertain future. To stay the same meant destruction. Finally, it was one man, Nachshon, who put his foot into the water, took the risk, and moved to the future. The Jewish future required risk, just as ours does. Nothing remains the same. Change is a positive Jewish value. We are empowered to "go forth," to risk moving into our future, and, sometimes, to change our very identity.

Changing the course of our life, being open to new experiences, and having the courage to risk moving from the status quo, often involve a spiritual going forth. In our search for meaning in life, we are given the freedom to change how we see our own self and our own spirituality. Daniel Gordis looks at the passage of Genesis 12 and the instruction *lech l'cha* (go forth) and offers this intriguing three-part analysis that encompasses the search for the spiritual in all of us:

> First, God's relationship with Abram begins outside of the Promised Land; each of us begins our adult spiritual journey unsatisfied, not where we ultimately wish to be. Second, God instructs Abram to risk virtually everything he knows and loves for the possibility of a greater, richer, more nurturing spiritual life; none of us should expect the search for spiritual fulfillment to be simple or mechanical. We, too, will have to risk. Third, God requires the Jewish people to wander for forty years after they leave Egypt; our spiritual journeys are often not only difficult, but also lengthy. When we seek the spiritual, we dare not expect instant gratification. (Gordis 1995, p. 44)

Risking to move forward with our lives, being willing to keep searching for new ideas and challenges—these are all part of the world in which we are now entering. It is a process that spans a lifetime. Judaism is an approach to life that affirms our ability to continue to evolve as human beings, no matter how many years we have lived.

Sometimes, the change and risk do not involve literally moving your life to a different place and uprooting your family. Sometimes, as Jacob demonstrates in Genesis 32, growth and change take place within your soul, within the relationship you have with your own self. Genesis 32 finds Jacob returning to his native land. He had fled to Haran after he received his brother Esau's birthright blessing from their father, Isaac. He now returns, older and perhaps humbled as a result of his experiences with his father-in-law, Laban. He is made aware that Esau is near and has brought his army. How will Jacob respond? Time and circumstances have changed him. We see Jacob send his entourage away. He is at the River Jabbok and stands alone, at night, confronting his past and his future and, in truth, his very self. Each of us, many times in our lives, come to camp at our own River Jabbok. Like Jacob, we meet again the reality of being *l'vado*: We are there alone, and we wrestle with the past as we attempt to chart a future. And each of us, like Jacob, emerges scarred and changed, we hope for the better. The story of Jacob wrestling at the Jabbok is one of the great moments in biblical literature. You can almost see the action as if it were being staged, the stage dark except for the spotlight illuminating this man who faces his brother after years of estrangement. What will he find? Who has Esau become? Who has Jacob become? It is as if the spirit of *ayecha* imbues the scene. And Jacob is *l'vado*, alone, as the word reappears in the text.

Now Jacob was left alone, and a man (*ish*) wrestled with him until the rise of dawn. When [the man] saw that he could not overcome him, he struck Jacob's hip-socket, so that Jacob's hip-socket was wrenched as [the man] wrestled with him. Then he said, "Let me go; dawn is breaking!" But [Jacob] said, "I will not let you go unless you bless me!" The other said to him, "What is your name?" and he said,

"Jacob." "No more shall you be called Jacob, but Israel, for you have struggled with God and with human beings, and you have prevailed." (Genesis 32:25–29)

Who does Jacob wrestle with? Who do we wrestle with as we contemplate changes in our lives? Who is this *ish* who confronts Jacob? Dr. Norman J. Cohen of the Hebrew Union College writes that Jacob was confronting all of his past, all the aspects of his life, both human and divine: "That night, all the parts of Jacob and all the parts of his life came together, and he would never be the same" (Norman J. Cohen 1998, p. 105).

Another contemporary scholar, Carol Ochs, sees in the combination of traditional interpretations a similar goal—the need for Jacob to take responsibity for his actions and life: "During Jacob's night alone, he wrestles with God, as some say; or with an angel, according to others; or with his unresolved relationship with his brother, as still others maintain. These three interpretations may well amount to the same thing, because wrestling with God is facing the truth, wrestling with an angel is fighting with a messenger of his truth, and wrestling with our unresolved relationships is looking within and taking responsibility for our actions" (Ochs 2001, p. 57). The result of the struggle is, of course, a transformation of Jacob. This is symbolized by the change in his name from Jacob to Israel (Genesis 32:28). In order to receive this blessing, Jacob must release the *ish* with whom he had struggled. In other words, a key aspect of Jacob's transformation is letting go.

Life is a series of "letting go" opportunities. From the moment we are born to the moment we die, no matter in what stage of life we find ourselves, we are in constant flux. We are always transitioning, or at least have the potential to do so. We leave the womb and the breast. We leave the security of home for school and gradually "let go" of those ties. How many of us remember the time when we had to "let go" of children? The memory of standing on the bimah at our child's bar or bat mitzvah, the time our children drove away from us for the first time, letting go of more control as they celebrated what they thought was independence. That "letting go" when we drove or flew home from dropping this child off at his dormitory for that first semester at college and the remarkable change in him when he returned for his first Thanksgiving. There is the "letting go" of a child at her wedding, the "letting go" of a parent or perhaps a friend or, God forbid, a child, at a funeral. There is the "letting go" that we all will undergo as we let go of some of what we were able to do when we were younger. Our journey is a story of "letting go" and moving on, and in that journey, there is the need for faith—faith to let go and move on. In this sense we are all Abraham, considering the challenge to "go forth"; and Jacob, as we wrestle with our own dreams and demons. And all too often we face these challenges and opportunities *l'vado*!

Think about the many times you have had to "let go" and how you felt in between the safety of the known and the wonder of the unknown. Dr. Dan Gottlieb is a psychologist, columnist, and radio talk-show host in the Philadelphia area. He and I were talking a while ago on a radio show, and I asked for his take on the idea that we are always, in a way, "letting go." Dan paused for a second and then quietly said that moving away from past identities is painful and frightening. "Letting go," he continued, "is always a positive thing; grasping onto anything causes pain, we suffer if we try and hold on . . . when we let go we literally open ourselves up" (Gottlieb 2009). Many of us, in recent years, have had to face the challenge of reinventing ourselves. Some of this has been voluntary;

we finally have the time to do what we want. For some, it has been a case of economic restructuring, which has led to the uncertainty of the unknown, of what to do next, of what this uncertain future will hold. For some, the need to reinvent ourselves has been caused by a change in primary relationships: a death, a divorce, or a separation. We find we must negotiate the wilderness of "letting go" before we can arrive at our next stop. And always that tension—do I go forth, or do I stay? "At several points we will ask, Should I go? Should I stay? At several turning points—with our parents, our friends, our partners in passion, our partners in marriage—we will struggle with questions of intimacy and autonomy. How far can I go and still be connected? What can I—and do I—want to do for myself? And exactly how much of me am I prepared to give up for love, or simply for shelter? At several points in our life, we may insist: I'll do it myself. I'll live by myself. I'll solve it myself. I'll make my own decisions. And, having made *that* decision, we may find ourselves scared to death of standing alone" (Viorst 1986, p. 46). Yet, as we look forward, we know that a future of standing still is a future of stagnation. A Sacred Aging project survey respondent named Rick wrote about looking forward from his own experience: "I would stress the importance and possibility of constant and ever continual reinvention. We are unlimited in our potential to learn and grow. None of us need continue in paths that have ceased to be meaningful and fruitful."

Lech l'cha, letting go and moving on, requires us to let go of "what was" and move forward to "what will be." A moment or moments of the unknown accompany these transitions. What sustains us in those moments of tension and concern is often faith—faith in a future, faith in our own innate sense of self and worth, and faith in the mystery of God. Along with these powerful forces, many of our survey respondents were clear in emphasizing the relationships with friends, family, and their own religious community. The fact that the synagogue was a real "caring community" often supported their transitions and made "letting go" less lonely. Gerry, one of the Sacred Aging survey respondents, affirmed this as he wrote: "I have been able to accept life changes (including the loss of my parents recently), and move forward. My synagogue family has helped make these transitions easier, through support of my network of synagogue friends, and sharing what we are going through in our own lives." There is no standing still in life; there is only transition and change. Judaism gives us the freedom and permission to embrace those changes and transitions, whether they are personal or communal, familial or societal. And Judaism also recognizes that these transitions are fraught with tension and fear, for there are moments when we are truly *l'vado* and when we wrestle with all our demons and doubts. In the end, however, we often reflect what Marcia, a woman in her eighth decade wrote: "I manage to not 'let go,' but 'keep going.' There really isn't a choice! As others have said before me, we do what we have to do."

This "letting go" and moving forward dance is something we rarely speak about or even consider. My friend Rabbi Jake Jackofsky (z"l) introduced me to a powerful poem by our colleague, the passionate and prophetic Rabbi Harold Schulweis of Los Angeles. The poem is called "Holding On and Letting Go" and has a theme of life and death and what we can take from a life. Within the poem is a wonderful and powerful image of the trapeze artist, who lets go of the bar and is suspended in air, alone, waiting and having faith that the next bar of the trapeze will be where it is supposed to be. I have used that image in teaching this idea of "letting go" and moving on. Its imagery resonates with many who can identify what it has meant for them to "let go" of the security of the "bar" and have faith that they will move confidently into a good future. It is in that aloneness that we all wrestle with our own selves and our own attempt to answer God's *ayecha?*

Holding On and Letting Go

Hold on and let go.
On the surface of things
           contradictory counsel.
But one does not negate the other.
The two are complementary, dialectical
           two sides of one coin.
Hold on—death is not the final word
The grave no oblivion.
Hold on in Kaddish, Yahrzeit, Yizkor.
No gesture, no kindness, no smile
           evaporates—
Every kindness, every embrace
has its afterlife
           in our minds, our hearts, our hands.
Hold on and let go.
Sever the fringes of the tallit of the deceased
the knot that binds us to the past.
Hold on
Not enslaving memory that sells the future
           to the past
nor recollection that makes us passive,
listless, resigned.
But memory that releases us
           for new life.

Lower the casket, the closure meant
to open again the world
of new possibilities.
Return the dust to the earth
not to bury hope
but to resurrect the will to live
Artists, aerialists
on a swinging trapeze
> *letting go one ring to catch another*
> *to climb to higher heights.*
Hold on and let go
> *a courageous duality*
> *that endows our life*
> *with meaning.*
>> *Neither denying the past*
>> *nor foreclosing the future.*
The flow of life
> *the divine process*
> *gives and takes*
 retains and creates.
Old and new yesterday and tomorrow
> *both in one embrace.*
The Lord giveth and the Lord taketh
> *Blessed be the name of the Lord.*
>> (Schulweis 1990, pp. 304–5)

Chapter 4 ────────────────────

THE GOD
OF OUR FUTURE?

*Moses said to God, "When I come to the Israelites and say
to them, 'The God of your ancestors has sent me to you,'
and they ask me, 'What is his name?' what shall I say
to them?" And God said to Moses, "Ehyeh-Asher-Ehyeh,"
continuing, "Thus shall you say to the Israelites,
'Ehyeh sent me to you.'"* EXODUS 3:13–14

וַיֹּאמֶר מֹשֶׁה אֶל־הָאֱלֹהִים הִנֵּה אָנֹכִי בָא אֶל־בְּנֵי
יִשְׂרָאֵל וְאָמַרְתִּי לָהֶם אֱלֹהֵי אֲבוֹתֵיכֶם שְׁלָחַנִי
אֲלֵיכֶם וְאָמְרוּ־לִי מַה־שְּׁמוֹ מָה אֹמַר אֲלֵהֶם:
וַיֹּאמֶר אֱלֹהִים אֶל־מֹשֶׁה אֶהְיֶה אֲשֶׁר אֶהְיֶה
וַיֹּאמֶר כֹּה תֹאמַר לִבְנֵי יִשְׂרָאֵל אֶהְיֶה שְׁלָחַנִי
אֲלֵיכֶם:

Vayomer Moshe el-HaElohim hineih anochi va el b'nei
Yisrael v'amarti lahem Elohei avoteichem sh'lachani
aleichem v'amru li ma sh'mo ma omar aleihem.
Vayomer Elohim el Moshe Ehyeh Asher Ehyeh
vayomer ko tomar liv'nei Yisrael ehyeh sh'lachani aleichem.

JUDAISM URGES US TO CONTINUE TO GROW AND FUL-
fill our own potential. There is a dynamic aspect, I believe, in being created in the "image and likeness" of
God. Part of that dynamism is an understanding that, as we age,

57

our relationship to God also evolves. We model being a *tzelem*, a reflection of God, through the relationships we have with others and with ourself. Those relationships must evolve and mature, or else face stagnation and decay. So too with our relationship with that mystery we call God. The vehicle for expressing that evolving relationship is often through the reinterpretation and creation of religious rituals.

Exodus 3:14 reminds us of our ever-changing understanding of God. Moses was tending his father-in-law Jethro's flock when he was confronted by the bush that burned but was not consumed. It was time for Moses to assume leadership. Already anticipating a challenge on the part of the Israelites to his newfound relationship with God, Moses asks for God's name. God instead responds with a cryptic description: *Ehyeh Asher Ehyeh*. The dialogue in Exodus 3 reminds us that our relationship with God is fluid and changeable, and that we come to understand God in our lives in many different ways, depending on the context of the life we are living at any given time. There are times when we are unable to "hear" God's call. Then there are times when we become open to it, when things take place in our lives that change who we are and what we are able to "hear." That is one of the reasons why I feel that modern translations of Exodus 3:14 do not translate the Hebrew *Eyheh Asher Ehyeh* as a static "I am Who I am," but leave the phrase as it is, implying that our relationships and definitions of God are open to change and interpretation. Our relationship with God is ongoing, expanding, and changing. When we "define" God, we limit God. Heschel reflects on this openness when he writes: "An idea of a theory of God can easily become a substitute for God. This is why I have always been careful not to define God in terms of one idea. God in search of man is an *ongoing process*.

It is not a notion; it is a process. The prophets had no *idea* of God. What they had was an understanding" (Heschel 1996, p. 162). The dynamism of this belief is seen in the prayer book. For centuries, Jews have recited prayers that include the phrase "God of Abraham, God of Isaac, and God of Jacob." Contemporary prayer books add "God of Sarah, God of Rebecca, God of Rachel, and God of Leah." Commentators have taught that this type of repetition is done purposely to teach us that God is redefined in every generation. This reminds us that we are given permission to doubt, challenge, and redefine what God means for us in each stage of our lives: "God's essence, or at least our perception of it, is always in the process of forming, perpetually developing" (Gordis 1995, p. 183). As we "go forth" and risk confronting what God means for us as we age, we are given permission to let go of past beliefs that are often rooted in myth, superstition, and childhood fantasies. We are challenged to not fear a dialogue with meaning: "In focusing more on 'relationship with God' than 'belief in God' Judaism differs from other Western religious traditions. While some Christian communities urge their followers, 'believe and you will be saved,' Judaism's rough equivalent is 'search and you will find meaning'" (Gordis 1995, p. 55). In this, Gordis reflects the mood of much of Jewish tradition. It is in the searching for God that we find our place in the universe, and this is an ongoing, lifelong process. Our own aging process and our own life experience propel us to seek a more mature expression of God and a relationship with the sacred that has been forged and fashioned by our own life journeys. Baby boomers are challenging beliefs and practices that no longer resonate with where we are and who we are.

To remain dynamic, relationships—whether they are with other people or with God—must be in a state of motion. They will stagnate and die unless they are given the freedom to grow and evolve. Part of being *m'vakshim* is the understanding that life is lived in motion, in a constant state of psychospiritual tension that produces growth. Change is part of living, and as many of us have learned through our own experiences in life, certainty is often illusory:

> The phrase "relationship with God" is instructive because "relationship" does not imply certainty. "Relationship" implies gradual growth and learning with fits and starts, with periods of tremendous progress as well as deeply frustrating and painful times. Relationships develop, often unpredictably; Judaism's conception of how Jews come to know God is very similar. It is not certainty that Jews seek; Jewish life is about searching for God's sheltering nearness, a sense of God's presence, a glimpse of God's love. It is not an even, easy or predictable road, but it is open to believers and doubters alike. (Gordis 1995, p. 55)

Part of the gift of this open road of belief is that there is no limit or condition of time. As biblical stories such as the Burning Bush or Jacob's ladder (Genesis 28) remind us, God is always present; it is we who are often so closed to the possibility of the sacred that we cannot see or hear the Divine. I think that the story of the Burning Bush is also telling us that these moments of meaning arise not from grand or "aha" experiences, but from the quiet interactions between people. Perhaps that is why the call to Moses comes through an ordinary bush: "Sometimes, the call of the Other comes from the most unlikely of places, when we least expect it. But if we open our hearts and minds, we may be lucky enough to realize that the *sneh*, the lowly bush, is Sinai. Sinai is all around us; God is always there for us, calling to us" (Norman J. Cohen 2003, p. 70). God is calling *ayecha*, yet too often we hide, as Adam and Eve did in Genesis 3. As we become more aware of our own mortality, as our own aging impacts us, we tend to see the world in a new light.

For many of us, "God talk" has been alien and uncomfortable. We have never been given permission to talk about God, or even the vocabulary with which to start the conversation. Too many of us are burdened by a God concept that we last discussed as we prepared for a bar or bat mitzvah or argued over with a roommate in college. Those days are long gone. We are far different people than we were then, and it is folly to assume that the relationship we may have had with God then is at all useful to the stage in life where we are now. Jewish tradition embraces our search for a relationship with God that relates to our experiences, for a belief that provides support and, when needed, comfort. As with any vital relationship, this search is not static. It may also never provide answers to certain questions. That is one of the great challenges for us: to come to terms with the fact that in our searching for a relationship of meaning with God, we may never find all the answers we seek. The *why* of so much may be hidden from us. As we mature, we become aware that part of the mystery of existence is the fact that we have to accept that, for some issues and events, there may be no rational answer. As *m'vakshim*, our seeking may be the only reason we find, an end in itself. There are things that we may not ever understand.

Ehyeh Asher Ehyeh calls on us to develop a mature sense of our own spirituality. This may be one of the great challenges for the aging baby boomers. It is an acceptance that there are things in life that remain beyond our control. In accepting this, we gain a sense of liberation on a spiritual level. It may, as many of our survey respondents noted, free up one's soul to focus on the challenge of living life to the fullest, of accepting life's blessings, and of seeking meaning in the moment. I think one of the reasons we are seeing a surge in spiritual experimentation, new ritual creation, variations in traditional religious themes, and a greater acceptance of religious diversity lies in our desire to have our religiosity mature along with us. James Hollis, in his book *Finding Meaning in the Second Half of Life*, urges us to develop what he calls a "mature spirituality." This is a relationship with God that frees us from the infantilized beliefs and relationships with religion that all too often inhibit real growth. A mature spirituality propels us to see God not as an idealized parent, but as an internalized model of how to live a life of holiness. It is not a restrictive or controlling set of externally imposed rules, but a set of beliefs and practices, forged through our own life experience, that provides a foundation for moving forward in life. It is, perhaps, the difference between how we see the world as a child and how we see and experience the world as a still-evolving adult. Hollis notes that we have two major tasks as we age. The first is to recover a sense of personal authority, which he sees as determining what is true for us and to live it. With this task goes the challenge of finding or discovering a personal spirituality, the type of relationship with God that reflects who we are and how we live. He acknowledges that this task is not easy, and indeed the search for a mature spirituality may never end: "A mature spirituality," writes Hollis, "will seldom provide us with answers, and necessarily so, but will instead ask ever larger questions of us. Larger questions will lead to a larger life. A mature spirituality is critical for the second half of life because if we do not address these questions directly, chances are we will be living in subjugation to received values which delude, divert, or diminish us. . . . Any spirituality that keeps people in bondage to fear, to *tradition*, or to anything other than that which is validated by their personal experience is doing violence to the soul . . . Growing up spiritually means that we are asked to sort through the possibilities for ourselves, find what resonates for us, what is confirmed by our experiences not the consensus of others, and be willing to stand for what has proved true for us. For this reason, the twin tasks of finding personal authority and finding a mature spirituality are inextricably linked" (Hollis 2005, pp. 185–86). We are given a unique chance to address the creation of our mature spirituality every year during the High Holy Days. Perhaps the most powerful of the prayers during that span is the *Un'taneh Tokef*, which describes the ways God will decide "who shall live and who shall die." The language of the prayer is riveting, for it forces the worshiper to consider the issue of who controls what in life. When I read this prayer as a younger person, I thought it was so depressing and so unreal. How could a God somewhere decide the course of the coming year's events, even up to how people will die? As we experience more of life, however, the words become clearer. The poetry of the prayer is understood symbolically. The message I now teach about this prayer is that it is an intense reminder that we control very little in life. The experiences of our life become the fires in which we are tested to create our own personal, and thus maturing, spirituality. The myth of control is prevalent in Western society. It is a product of our industrial age and gives us the idea that no matter what the problem, if we just spend enough money or hire enough people we can control events or solve that problem. Many of us recognize that this is true only up to a point. So much of life we cannot control. As we attempt to search for our own relationship with God, our own place in this universe, our own spiritual path, we come to realize that there will be things that we may never understand. There will be events that we cannot control, no matter how much money we spend on them or how many committees study them. This acceptance of our own imperfection, or our own humanity, can allow us to see something greater in the journey of our life: its mystery. Perhaps, as we age, we become more accepting of the fact that life is not a problem to be solved, "but a mystery to be lived" (Kurtz and Ketcham 1992, p. 128). Moses stood at the Burning Bush and came to accept his life's work, his mission, his passion. He asked God for a name to tell the Children of Israel and the answer came back *Ehyeh Asher Ehyeh*. In that moment God told Moses to go forward, to live and experience life and have faith, and in doing so God's name will become known. That same opportunity exists for us as our next stage of life unfolds. We have the opportunity to be open to God, to revisit and redefine our relationship with God, to celebrate that "mystery" and to search for our voice in this covenant with the sacred. We are being called to reexamine our relationship with God. Faith is not security and comfort; faith is doubt, movement, dialogue—a dialectical process that involves belief, life experience, and the evolution of new beliefs in light of that experience: "Faith is not a system but an on-going striving for faith, involving acceptance of perplexity, joy of devotion as well as the agony of doubt, moments of illumination as well as groping in the darkness of vapidity" (Heschel 1972, p. 199).

The relationship we have with God may never be fully understood. Yet, the sense of the Sacred is always there, if we but open our eyes to see. In doing so, we may come to understand that the mystery of God's presence is a constant; it is we who change. It is a major leap of faith for most of us to willingly surrender the rational side of our self, the "how" side of our being, to accept that there is something beyond our own experience that is always with us, if we but wish or choose to see it. Take, for example, the story of the man walking on a beach: Whenever he looked behind him, he saw his footprints, accompanied by a second set alongside his own. He was comforted, for he knew God was walking with him. Along the way, he fell into misfortune. He looked behind and was greatly troubled, for he saw only one set of footprints. He called out to God: "How could you abandon me in my time of trouble?" He then heard a voice respond: "I have not abandoned you—I am carrying you."

The primary means by which we express our relationship with God is through our religious rituals. Rituals help carry us through life's transitions. Longevity is producing new stages of life, and in a desire to infuse these new stages with spiritual meaning, boomers are at the forefront of re-visioning and revising religious rituals that, like our relationship with God, evolve and change. Rituals are one of the ways through which we expand and explore our understanding of our own existence. They help link an individual to a moment, a community, and to that mystery that exists beyond oneself. Rituals reinforce that we exist within a certain context and history, and that by formally celebrating or recognizing an event in our life, we and the event take on additional meaning. Rituals create a relationship between the participant and the event that can transcend the ordinary: "All rituals have an important relationship component. They help us to 'see' what's going on in relationships, and offer a specific time and place to highlight ongoing relationships and to make relationship changes" (Imber-Black and Roberts 1992, p. 30). Our own aging involves understanding loss, on the one hand, and celebrating new aspects of consciousness, on the other. There is a sense of personal liberation in our transitions that can be enhanced and, indeed, made sacred, by placing them in the context of religious rituals. The extension of life span and the reality that much of that longevity can be healthy and productive reminds us of the value of creating moments of sacred possibility for this longevity revolution. Rituals can connect us to our traditions, reinforce the value of community, provide meaning for what is being commemorated or experienced, and, most importantly, celebrate the necessity and the power of being in relationships with other people as well as with the transcendent meaning of our existence. Longer life spans have opened the door to the creation of new rituals that imbue meaning to new life stages.

This dimension of ritual creation has led to discussions of the issue of transformation. Many view transformation as one of the key elements in religious ritual. Ritual allows individuals to transition from one phase of life to another, often liberating them for change. For rituals, like relationships, must be open to evolution and change: "In other words, rituals belong to human history. Ritual process belongs to historical process. It is not some kind of detached thing remote from the events that it influences. Agents of transformation, rituals are themselves transformed by the histories to which they belong" (Driver 1991, p. 184). Our aging is now providing opportunities to aid in this process of personal and cultural transformation by creating new rituals that respond to lifestyles and life stages that may be different than those of previous generations. The search for our own answers to God's *ayecha* can be enhanced and given texture through the development or adaptation of rituals that speak to the experiences and stages through which we are now living. For many members of the baby boom generation, long at the forefront of the transformation and adaptation of contemporary Judaism, there is a hunger for meaning and a realization that rituals can help provide that sense of meaning and connection, or relationship to other people and to the mystery of that which is beyond our self:

> The rites of birth, puberty, marriage and death enable us to move through life's stages with a clearer understanding of the changes taking place in ourselves, in our relationship to others and in our relationship to God. The emergence of new stages or substages creates a need for new rituals to help us move with greater ease and purpose through transitional events.
>
> The rapid graying of faith communities and dramatically increased life expectancy lend import to the development of rites that give shape and meaning to these new stages and mark the passage through the Third Age. The most effective rituals are those that emerge from and give meaning and purpose to the life of a community. (Robb 1994, p. 8)

Some new rituals have emerged from workshops and seminars that asked people for specific suggestions about the kind of rituals they would wish to have for significant moments. These discussions often involved the desire to have a blessing or ritual that thanked God for allowing the individual to get through a difficult time, usually associated with illness and recovery. This pointed to the need to teach that such blessings already exist within our tradition and need to be reinterpreted and brought into greater use. The *gomel* blessing is one such example. It is a traditional blessing recited when someone has passed through a difficult period or survived a dangerous journey or a life-threatening situation. The blessing thanks God "who has bestowed every goodness upon me," to which the congregation responds: "Amen, may the One who has bestowed goodness upon you continue to bestow every goodness upon you forever." Now this blessing is being used to sanctify moments when people emerge from a particularly dangerous operation or illness or threat to their life.

Many new rituals have been drawn from the Jewish feminist movement of recent decades. Take, for example, the *Simchat Chochmah* ceremony, which celebrates the attainment of wisdom. This ceremony has been performed by individuals in synagogues at a significant birthday. It is designed to recognize a sense of maturity, a sense that the celebrant has lived awhile and has now learned to understand how the world works, what is important in life, and how that person can make a significant contribution to the world. Most of all, it celebrates life and looks ahead to the unfolding of even greater experiences that will be supported *by wisdom only accumulated by experience.* A portion of one such *Simchat Chochmah* ritual contains this expression of thanks and anticipation:

> River of light and truth, You have sustained me these many years and brought me to this place in my life's journey. Let me look out with wisdom, from the high ground of my years and experiences, over the terrain of my life. Let me gaze out toward the past and the future with a heightened sense of Your presence as my Guide. Let me see that growth is not reserved for any one season, and that love and fulfillment are not the exclusive province of the young. (Address and Rosenkranz 2005, p. 61)

People are asking rabbis for new rituals to mark significant moments. Are these rituals for everyone? Perhaps not. Do we run the risk of demeaning the power of ritual if people begin to develop what some would call "private" rituals? This is something that we must examine. Will this trend decline? I think not, for we seem to be in such need of finding meaning for our lives that the exploration of rituals can be the means through which individuals rediscover their own need for spiritual meaning. For example, consider the creation of a ritual for the removal of a wedding ring following the traditional year of mourning. Several years ago I was involved in a discussion with a colleague who had been asked by one of his congregants to create a ritual during which the widower would remove his wedding ring. He asked that the ceremony be done in private, on the same bimah on which, over a quarter of a century earlier, he and his wife had been married. The rabbi had a long and cherished relationship with this man and his wife, knew of the depth of their love, and appreciated that this man was seeking a means by which he could "move on." Is such a ceremony for everyone? No. However, after the rabbi and his congregant processed the reasons for this request, they developed a ritual that allowed the congregant to stand with his rabbi in the sanctuary and remove the ring. Part of the ritual that was created for this man and for this moment follows:

> *With this ring I was betrothed to you,*
> *According to the laws of Moses, Miriam, and Israel.*
> *Ecclesiastes teaches me that there is a time for everything,*
> *Especially for birth and death.*
> *From our heritage I learned the importance of reaffirming our*
> *faith*

Even at the most difficult of times,
Even when in the Valley of the Shadow of Death.
With the removal of this ring, I acknowledge again
That I am losing your companionship.
But the memories and love will always remain
Dear to my heart.
May they continue as an inspiration to me
And to those you touched.
May they remain a blessing,
And may we always praise God
For the gifts of life and patience,
And for the righteous judgments made.
God asks that we walk in the way of Torah
May that continue to be my will.
Amen.

(Address and Rosenkranz 2005, p. 69–70)

As life spans increase and health is maintained, an increasing number of us will find ourselves in a situation of being alone, either through divorce or the death of a spouse. In the process of living our life, we may be fortunate to meet someone with whom we wish to share the rest of our life. Yet, due to what may be a wide variety of circumstances, marriage is not desirable or appropriate. The growing reality of older-adult cohabitation is going to demand that clergy and their denominations consider developing different types of pre-relationship counseling. Two people come to their clergyperson and ask for a blessing that will sanctify their relationship. People in their sixties, seventies, eighties, and beyond, who are making these requests, bring adult children, established

estates, grandchildren, and, often, years of living alone and doing things "their way." Likewise, there is the challenge of what
will happen if one partner gets ill and the other, who perhaps had
years of intense caregiving with a previous spouse, opts out of the
relationship with no legal recourse. There are a host of these and
related issues that should be discussed prior to officiating at such
a cohabitation ceremony. Yet we are charged with the challenge
of facing this new reality and offering some means of sanctifying
the gift of intimacy as people age. Having found love and security with a caring partner, they may need to thank God that they
have found each other and ask for peace and comfort for however
many years they may be granted. Genesis 2:18 reminds us that it
is not good for us to be alone. These rituals are not marriages and
many clergy have indicated a reluctance to be part of them so that
the clergyperson, or Judaism could not be construed as having affirmed cohabitation without marriage. The reality, however, is that
these types of living arrangements are no longer unusual and, in
my opinion, will be a growing reality as boomers age. In many of
these relationships we observe opportunities to develop something
sacred for people who come to their congregation or clergyperson
to seek a blessing for health, life, and love. There is no blessing
in being alone or living in isolation. The desire for intimacy with
another human being is a need that all of us share, no matter what
our age. It becomes even stronger as we age. There is comfort and
blessing in being in relationship with another human being, as the
following selection from one such ceremony attests:

May they be healthy and lead productive lives.
May they find sustenance in their relationship.

May they find enjoyment in each other.
May their physical presence strengthen their spiritual growth.
May they nurture their fragility and rely on their strengths.
May their days be full, and inundated with love.
Amen.

(Address and Rosenkranz 2005, p. 63)

There are numerous other examples of rituals and blessings being developed and in use that reflect various aspects of the new longevity. The Sacred Aging project of the Union for Reform Judaism has monitored a wide variety of examples. Some are used to welcome people into assisted-living facilities, or to support a couple or individual transitioning from the "family" home, downsizing from the home where a family may have been raised to a smaller dwelling. There are rituals being developed for the onset of menopause. One of the most challenging areas of ritual development reflects the reality that with more people living longer, we may be about to experience a growth in cases of dementia and Alzheimer's disease. We are now seeing the beginning of discussion within our community of the following scenario, which is being played out with increasing frequency.

In workshops that I have conducted on ritual creation as part of the Sacred Aging project, invariably we hear the case, often presented by the clergy, where a congregant comes to her clergyperson to seek guidance. The congregant has been caring for her spouse, who now resides in an Alzheimer's facility. The congregant visits regularly, cares for the spouse, and loves the spouse. Yet, the congregant also understands that her spouse is never coming home and, in fact, "isn't really my spouse any more." On a trip designed to give this caregiver a break, she meets someone and strikes up a friendship. The friendship grows and becomes intimate. The congregant comes to speak with the clergyperson out of a deep sense of anguish. What is she feeling? Guilt? Is she committing adultery? The congregant finds it difficult or impossible to discuss the situation with her grown children and certainly difficult to discuss with the circle of friends with whom the couple have shared so much of life. But, this wife asks, "is it wrong for me? I have my needs as well and I am still a vibrant, healthy person, and who knows how long this long journey will last?" There is no talk of abandoning the person suffering with Alzheimer's, yet the congregant argues that, given the nature and duration of the illness, should she not be allowed to find someone with whom she can share part of her life and find a measure of intimacy and support?

The psychological and spiritual tolls may be onerous and, as you might expect, there is no unanimity among religious communities on this subject. (Mundy 2009). Can we provide some sense of comfort, guidance, and caring that is rooted in Jewish tradition? Given the realities of extended life spans and the unique and frightening aspects of these cases, do we now need to look at redefining such terms as "adultery"? Should congregations create opportunities for this scenario to be discussed from within the context of Jewish tradition, medical technology, and the psychospiritual pressures that ensue? Should Jewish communities, denominations, or individual congregations create a ritual or document that addresses this situation, a document that would be signed by both husband and wife, reviewed periodically, and discussed with their clergyperson? Is there a need for a document that recognizes the horrible and tragic circumstances of a person being afflicted by a long bout of dementia or Alzheimer's disease and gives permission for the spouse to seek physical or emotional or spiritual companionship outside the marital relationship?

There have been attempts to come up with just such rituals and documents. Some conversations have taken place concerning the challenge or possibility of redefining the traditional concept of the *pilegesh* (the concubine) and reinterpreting it to allow for these kinds of scenarios. Another approach seeks to redefine the traditional concept of the *agunah* in order to provide guidance in this uncharted area. (A traditional concept, *agunah* derives from Ruth 1:13, meaning "restrained" or "cut off." It refers to the situation in which a wife has been left alone, not having heard from her husband for a long period. She is prevented from remarrying. The husband's disappearance or lack of presence prevents her from obtaining a bill of divorce, a *get*, and thus she is in a type of legal limbo.) As part of a Sacred Aging class at the Hebrew Union College–Jewish Institute of Religion, a colleague who created a ritual to deal with the Alzheimer's spouse issue calls it a "Ritual Commemorating Becoming an *Aguneh/Agunah* Due to Illness." Part of the ritual's introduction states:

> This ceremony acknowledges one's status as an *agunah*, . . . This ritual finds itself sitting in between several other rituals. It is close to divorce because it serves as a way of freeing an individual from certain bonds, but in other ways it serves as a renewal of marriage vows because it reaffirms the promise to take care of their partner. . . . The primary purpose of this ritual in not meant to give someone the authority to go out and seek an extramarital relationship, it is a way to ritually acknowledge that the person they married

is no longer present, even though their body is still very much alive. One is still anchored (*agunah*) to their partner and must ensure that their body and needs are continually taken care of. They may not desert them. However, because they are acknowledging that their partner is no longer present, this ritual simultaneously confirms that they are bound to their partner yet also free, to some degree, to find companionship with someone else if that situation presents itself. Because they are still married to their original partner, they are not able to remarry, and if they have a child with someone outside of that marriage, the child will be a *mamzer*. (Bazeley 2009)

The ritual contains a series of readings and paragraphs that outline the reality that the ritual is an "acknowledgment that the mind and essence of [the spouse] . . . whom you committed yourself to years ago can no longer be found despite the fact that his/her body is still alive." The ritual, which is designed to be done with the spouse and a rabbi, goes on to affirm the caregiver's commitment to care for the spouse who is ill and to "ensure that he/she has the resources that he/she needs to survive despite the fact that our lives now take different paths." Is such a ritual and document for everyone? Hardly. However, the reality that such a scenario is being lived now by many of our people, and will be lived by many more in the coming decades, does open the door for synagogues and denominations to address this real-life situation from within a sacred context. Yes, it does require some changes in thinking. Yes, it does require some shifts in the way we regard the meaning of relationships and even marriage. But can we, in good faith, ignore this?

There have even been attempts within the modern Orthodox community to examine situations when marriage is, in a sense, not marriage. Rabbi J. David Bleich, a leading modern Orthodox authority, looked at various interpretations of marriage in a 1999 article titled "Can There Be Marriage without Marriage?" Bleich was wrestling with the challenges to the traditional concept of the *agunah* brought about by contemporary Western culture. Bleich cites other authorities who attempted to construct legal loopholes for relationships that would not require the Jewish divorce document (the *get*) and raises the question: "If, however, an acceptable arrangement could be identified that would halachically legitimate a sexual relationship outside the framework of matrimony, the problem of a *get* might readily be resolved by supplanting marriage with an alternative relationship reflecting that arrangement" (Bleich 1999, p. 40). Bleich continues to discuss various interpretations of the concept of the concubine and, as one might expect, concludes that such arguments are not in keeping with halachic Judaism. However, the fact that such an article was written in the first place opens the possibility of further discussion.

Our longevity is challenging us continually to reimagine our relationship with others and, ultimately, with God. Rituals can provide us the spiritual currency for that journey. Alan Wolfe of Boston College reminds us that ritual is never static. He argues that the best way to understand this is to make the noun "ritual" into a verb "to capture the process by which individuals move in and out of transitions as they search for symbols and rituals that make sense out of their lives. . . . [T]he experiences of Jews in modern America teach everyone that traditions remain alive and well and they also teach that traditions, in this day and age, take forms that people who once lived in traditional societies would hardly be able to recognize" (Wolfe 2003, p. 110). Why are we so eager to create these new ritual moments? We do so because we need to be in relationship, with others at special moments and with that Mystery that lies beyond our own self. Rituals remind us that we have connections, that we are not *l'vado*, and that our existence and life have meaning. They point the way to holiness.

Chapter 5 ─────────────────────

THE HOLINESS
OF CAREGIVING

Speak to the whole Israelite community and say to them:
You shall be holy, for I, the Eternal your God,
am holy. LEVITICUS 19:2

דַּבֵּר אֶל־כָּל־עֲדַת בְּנֵי־יִשְׂרָאֵל וְאָמַרְתָּ אֲלֵהֶם
קְדֹשִׁים תִּהְיוּ כִּי קָדוֹשׁ אֲנִי יְהֹוָה אֱלֹהֵיכֶם:

Dabeir el kol adat b'nei Yisrael v'amarta aleihem:
K'doshim tih'yu ki kadosh ani Adonai Eloheichem.

PERHAPS NOTHING BETTER DESCRIBES OUR GEN-eration's greatest challenge than the life stage known as caregiver. We often enter this life stage unprepared and in an instant. Thanks to the blessings of medical technology, this stage can last months, years, or even decades. Some argue that, in the coming years, elder care may replace child care as the number-one family concern. Many of us know this already. My own story will resonate with many readers' own experiences. In the course of less than a decade, my mother went from independent living to assisted living and, following one quick event, to a skilled nursing facility that specializes in dementia. Her journey from self-reliance to dependence is not unusual. Her path from enjoying her evening cocktail to having to be fed by family and aides is a path now shared by many of our loved ones. We take that journey with them, juggling work, our own families, and our own lives, along with the necessity and mitzvah of being caregivers. So we sit with our loved ones and, in those quiet moments, often find our souls asking, "Where is God in this?" The "art" of caregiving places before us unique opportunities to search our own souls as we, in caring for others, come face to face with the reality of our own mortality. The call of *ayecha* takes on a deeper texture as we hold the hand of the one who held ours and feed the person who fed us.

We can begin to seek an answer to this call in one of the most significant and meaningful chapters of Torah, which sets the very foundation for Jewish ethics. Often called the Holiness Code, Leviticus 19 gives a clear and concise summary of Jewish life and offers us insight into how to approach the art of caregiving. Every aspect of life, from ritual observance to economic life, is covered within the chapter; and each statement is capped off with the recurring phrase *ani Adonai*, "I am God," echoing the key phrase at the beginning of the chapter: "You shall be holy, for I, the Eternal your God, am holy" (19:2). As we grow older and are more aware of the gift of life and the mystery of that gift, as we come to more deeply cherish the relationships that we have, and as we continue to search for our own sense of purpose, Judaism reminds us of the need to ground this awareness in a sense of holiness. Why? Because it is this sense of the sacred that makes us truly a *tzelem Elohim*, modeling the fundamental relationship that we have with God. From the first verse of the chapter, we receive instruction as to what our task is as human beings, as images of God: "The Torah here reveals in no uncertain terms what a human being's job description is. In essence, we are here on earth for no other purpose than to grow and blossom spiritually—to become holy. Our potential and therefore our goal should be to become as spiritually refined and elevated as is possible" (Morinis 2007, p. 10). Leviticus 19 reminds us that in doing the sacred work of caregiving, we are not alone. *Ani Adonai* is the foundation of developing a caregiving relationship that creates moments of meaning in the performance of the mitzvah of honoring and respecting our loved ones.

Caring for our parents, combined with our own aging and our caring for and involvement with children and grandchildren, has qualified many of us for membership in what has been called the "sandwich generation." In my work in congregations on this subject, I have learned that the term "club sandwich generation" is even more descriptive, for multigenerational caregiving is becoming the norm. It is no longer unusual for a sixty-something-year-old man or woman to be caring for a parent in his late eighties or nineties, while at the same time being very involved with a child in her late twenties or thirties, and at the same time, helping care for one or more grandchildren. All of this comes precisely when we thought we would be having "our time," free from burdens like these. The longevity revolution has changed the dynamics of many of our families and has raised the challenges of caregiving to new levels of intensity. Add to this mix the reality of long distances between parents and children, the continuing mobility of our culture, plus the economic challenges associated with caregiving, and you have a recipe for stress and strain: "In effect, the next twenty years will require a massive transfer of resources and people away from the care of children, who will decline in relative numbers, and toward the care of old people" (McArdle 2008, p. 82).

As noted earlier, elder care is replacing child care as the number-one family issue. While society at large may not have completely grasped this point, many of us are living it. With more people in need of caregiving and changes in family systems, we are seeing a more "vertical," or "beanpole," rather than "pyramid" caregiving system evolve. That is, more members of more generations are involved in caring for people: "No longer is there a single culturally dominant family pattern, but rather a multiplicity of family and household arrangements whose forms change frequently in response to changing personal and occupational circumstances" (Pruchno and Smyer 2007, p. 129). The Beatles wondered if anyone would care for us when we became sixty-four. Maybe they should have asked whom we would be caring for instead. We have become a generation of caregivers. Indeed, I suggest that we have made being a caregiver into a new life stage, a stage that comes on us usually in an instant. So how can we invest a sense of holiness into this role?

We read in Leviticus 19:32 that "you shall rise before the aged and show deference to the old; you shall fear your God: I am the Lord." The Hebrew word that is translated as "deference" (*yarei-tah*) shares a root with a word that appears in the beginning of the chapter in verse 3, in the context of respecting one's parents: "You shall each respect (*tira'u*) your mother and your father, and keep My sabbaths: I am the Eternal your God" (Leviticus 19:3). Three times in the Torah we are given the command to honor (*kabeid*) and respect (*tirah*) our parents (Exodus 20:12, Leviticus 19:3, and Deuteronomy 5:16). The Babylonian Talmud, in *Kiddushin* 31b–32a, records a discussion as to what these concepts mean. The Rabbis emphasize that in no way are we as caregivers to take away the dignity and sense of self-respect of any human being, no matter what their condition. They even ask if it is permissible to correct a parent in the midst of a discussion when you know the parent is not right. We are reminded throughout our tradition that the concept of respect is inviolable. People are human beings no matter what their condition or stage of life. We are not permitted to do anything that reduces a person's sense of dignity or self-respect.

In the Palestinian Talmud (*Kiddushin* 1:7) is a wonderful story of two men that is often used to teach this point. One gives his father plenty to eat and is said to inherit hell. The other puts his father to work in a mill and, as a result, inherits Eden. How could it be possible that the man who feeds his father "fattened chickens" is assigned to hell and the man who makes his dad work is rewarded? The Rabbis say that the first man simply ignores his dad, treats him with no sense of dignity, just says to him to be quiet, enjoy life, let me take care of you. The second man creates a situation wherein the father is working, contributing, and is protected from harm. The first son strips his father of his sense of dignity and worth; the second son affirms that dignity and worth.

These days, we aren't necessarily sending mom and dad off to the mill, but we do encounter, every day, situations in caring for an aging parent where these lessons apply. We'll go shopping, for example, at the supermarket. Mom and dad will give us a list, and we pick up the groceries on the way over for a visit. We unpack them and they ask "How much?" Our natural inclination is to say, "Don't worry about it," thinking that, after all, it is the right thing to do as mom and dad may be watching their expenses. The tradition, however, cautions us against making this a habit for, in doing so, we may gradually take away our parents' sense of self-respect, almost infantilizing them, making them feel totally dependent on us. The Talmud also provides us with an additional insight into the question of who pays for care. The Rabbis understood that we, the children, pay with time. Think about the time it may take to pick up mom, take her to her appointment at the clinic or for dialysis or chemotherapy. We drive and wait. We take her home, perhaps stopping on the way to fill a new prescription or share a bite to eat. Then we drop her home and make sure all is well. This can take hours, and the Talmud recognizes is as "paying":

> Though two opinions regarding who bears financial responsibility for an aged parent appear in the Talmud, the generally accepted preference was for the parent to pay for his or her food and clothing needs. This ruling stood in conflict with an older tradition which stated that children must honor their parents by spending on them. In order to maintain harmony between the two positions, the later Talmudic teachers claimed that the child's financial outlay took the form of loss of work time and profits it might bring. The child, then, was expected to help feed and clothe that parent if that was necessary. The food and clothing, however, was paid for by the parent. (Chernick 1987 , pp. 95–96)

Time and money can be a means of blessing or curse, compassion or control. The tradition offers us a guide for how to deal with this most delicate of dances. There are no rules, per se, in this. Each situation is different, and, as many of us know, a situation can change with almost no warning. In this new life stage of caregiving, we come face to face with the often-repeated verse in Leviticus 19, *ani Adonai* (I am God). There are moments of spiritual reckoning, awareness that some other power or mystery is present. They contain within them aspects of transcendence that are often frightening and almost always humbling. I speak of those quiet moments, private usually, when you are with the person being cared for. I am thinking of time spent with a parent, escorting her to a doctor's appointment, for example. You go around to her side of the car and help her out. You grab hold of her arm, or place your arm around her shoulder to help. And in a flash of insight, you are suddenly aware that this parent has become a frail older adult; that those arms that held you and cared for you now reach out to you for caring, support, and guidance. You experience a revelation, a sense that roles have changed; and you are humbled to realize the responsibility that is now yours. Many of us have had these moments. They are sacred and filled with awe. We become aware, ever so quietly, that there has been a shift in the relationship; and it is a time to thank God for the fact that we have been given the opportunity to be present in this transitional and revelatory experience. As powerful and spiritual as some of these moments may be, they are also fraught with psychic pain. These changes in roles are often met with frustration, anger, and sometimes acting out, depending on the circumstances and dynamics of the relationship involved. Our parent or loved one is confronted by having to "let go" of some independence and may find this frightening and debilitating.

We also undergo change. For these moments often raise within us fears of our own frailty and thoughts like, Will this be me in years to come? Who will care for me if and when I am in a similar situation? Perhaps, if we were better able to confront our own fears, we could be even more empathetic toward those for whom we care: "To care one must offer one's own vulnerable self to others as a source of healing. To care for the aging, therefore, means first of all to enter into close contact with your own aging self, to sense your own time, and to experience the movements of your own life cycle. From this aging self, healing can come forth and others can be invited to cast off the paralyzing fear for the future" (Nouwen 2005, p. 45).

It is also important to remember that some of us will practice this art of caregiving not for a parent, but for another family member: a spouse, a sibling, or even a child. These challenges are no less stressful, no less demanding, and provide comparable moments of spiritual growth. In times too terrible to contemplate, unless you live through them, there are often instances of quiet beauty and strength that reflect the pinnacle of what it means to be holy. I witnessed this over the course of a horrible summer. My close friend and colleague Rabbi "Jake" Jackofsky was diagnosed with a rare and fatal brain disease in June 2010. He came home from the hospital, and his wife was determined to manage his care, as long as possible, at home. With twenty-four-hour caregivers, and the support of dozens of friends and family, Jake remained at home. We spoke many times, on the phone and when I visited. Ellen, Jake's wife, was firm in her desire to keep her husband surrounded by the things that meant the most to him: his study, his books, his house, his dog, his friends, and his family, who were constantly present. Perhaps the most spiritual moment I witnessed was during a visit just three weeks before Jake's death, when he was bedridden and had great difficulty speaking. We all had dinner together in Jake's study, where his hospital bed had been placed. We brought trays into the study, and, as we sat there, Ellen leaned over Jake's bed and fed him dinner, speaking with him, holding him, touching him, just being present. This was an act of total devotion, motivated by deep love, which kept the promise of not allowing this man to be alone. As I observed this, there was no doubt in my mind that I was witnessing a profoundly spiritual moment. Even in such sadness, there is room for the sacred.

The challenge of caregiving can raise many issues within a family system, for not every situation has a solid foundation of family support and shared responsibility. There are times when the reality and necessity of following the fifth commandment brings up painful memories. The Torah commands us to "honor" and "respect" our parents, but we are not commanded to love them. This is one of the great insights of our tradition. We are commanded to love God, but we are given no comparable command to love our parents. Some of us must face the difficult situation of caring for an aging parent with whom we have been estranged. Every rabbi has had to counsel family members who are faced with this reality and who find it difficult to honor their parent in this way, given the lack of love, respect, and honor that had been afforded to them by that parent. What about situations of abandonment, abuse, and neglect? Are we still commanded to honor and respect our parents in those cases? The tradition seems to say yes. For that parent gave us life. But are there limits to this? Again, the tradition seems to come down on the side of reason, for it does make the statement that parents would forfeit the right to honor and respect if their behavior abrogated Jewish law and ethics: "Indeed, the commandments of respect and honor are incumbent upon children only when parents observe the commandments required of them. An attack upon the sources of Jewish values, the Torah, by the parent invalidates the parent's rights provided by that source. Parents who have been irresponsible, cruel, neglectful, and harmful to their children have failed to uphold their obligations in Jewish law and practice to their children. Hence, they have forfeited the 'honor' and 'respect' with which Jewish law entitles them" (Chernick 1987, p. 101).

Judaism, however, always holds out the hand of repentance. What if there is repentance on the part of the parent? In many families, time passes, circumstances change, and an opportunity arises for t'shuvah (repentance). Does this change the dynamic of responsibility? Rabbi Dayle A. Friedman presents us with an interesting possibility from our texts. She notes that Joseph Caro, in his major legal code of the mid-sixteenth century, the *Shulchan Aruch*, states that a child born out of wedlock is obligated to honor and respect a father, even if that father was a violator of law and a doer of evil. Friedman then notes that Moses Isserles, a European scholar who amended Caro's work for the Ashkenazi community, stated that the child is not obligated to honor the father unless the father repents:

> While Caro states that a parent's sinful behavior does not limit a child's obligations, Isserles suggests that a child is not obligated toward a parent who has transgressed laws or limits and failed to take responsibility for his or her actions. One way of harmonizing these views is to suggest that a child of an abusive parent is called to at least avoid doing anything active to hurt or dishonor a parent, but may not be obligated to provide direct care or take active measures to honor that parent. Thus, a child who has survived sexual abuse by her father could feel she has done the right thing by avoiding contact with him, while a son whose father is in recovery from alcoholism and has asked for his forgive-

ness might feel called to attend to his care needs. (Friedman 2003, p. 88)

I think that this scenario also points up the issue of competing values that often arises within the caregiving continuum. There is a part of us that may wish to "do the right thing." Yet, because of past family dynamics, that desire may come in conflict with personal history and cause undue stress and strain, and thus impact the caregiver's own health and the health and security of the caregiver's own family. The tradition is aware of the impact of stress within the caregiving dynamic. What guidance can we obtain from tradition for when mom or dad's situation just becomes too overwhelming for us to handle? How do we live so we do not lose our own "self" as we try to honor and respect our parent(s)? We want to do what is right, but things just spiral down in such a way that it becomes too burdensome, especially if we are juggling work, children, and spousal responsibilities. Is there ever a time when it is permissible to turn care and control over to a third party? Again, the tradition seems to anticipate what many of us are living through. Some commentators, including Maimonides in his *Mishneh Torah* of the twelfth century, argue that when it becomes too difficult, when the status quo may actually cause potential harm to the person being cared for and negatively impact the stability of our family system, it is permissible to cede control to the community or a third party. We know that there will come a time when the "right" thing to do is to bring in someone else to handle the caregiving responsibilities. Again, the idea of protecting and enhancing a parent-child relationship that is based on the values of *tzelem* becomes paramount: "Turning to a nursing home placement, in-home nursing services, or some part-time arrangement that relieves the child of fulltime caregiving is thus fully appropriate under Jewish law when the child's attempts to provide care will result only in a deterioration of the relationship, causing the child to manifest a lack of honor or reverence to the parent. The point at which this occurs will obviously vary from case to case, and each decision must be reached individually" (Langer 1998, p. 122).

The key in all these cases is context. Each situation must be judged on its own merits. No two families are the same; there is no template for any of this, no matter what anyone tries to say. Each set of family dynamics is particular to each family. Thus, when we find ourselves in these situations (and the majority of us will), we need to remind ourselves that we don't have to navigate these waters alone. An expanding number of agencies, individuals, and resources are trained and experienced in helping us make appropriate decisions. Make use of your clergyperson to help place these issues within a spiritual context that speaks to your particular situation. These caregiving situations can highlight the most meaningful aspects of our family relationships and point up possibilities to enhance the concept of *tzelem* with those with whom we have shared our lives.

Many of us in the first wave of the baby boom generation remember the great "causes" of our youth. We often recall those "good old days" when we were out protesting against the war in Vietnam or for equality in the civil rights movement or railing against those in the establishment who gave us Watergate. We often were in conflict with our parents over these issues, and many of us can remember heated "discussions" over a meal regarding these "causes." How curious, three-plus decades later, that our generations are not in conflict, but allies when it comes to issues like Social Security and Medicare, housing options, and the economics of caregiving. Hardly a day goes by without some doomsday warning from the government or an economist about the impending end of entitlement programs as we know them. Already health care and pension programs are being reevaluated and changed to reflect the new economics of aging. There may be no more pressing social justice cause emerging now than the cause of equality in health care and how entitlements can and will be distributed. This issue impacts every family across generational lines. With the shrinking number of younger workers who will contribute to entitlement programs, the issue of who will pay takes on an entirely new meaning. We have a challenge to become active in addressing these issues and ensuring an equitable solution for all of society. These discussions will not be easy, as the ongoing discussions on issues of health care and entitlement programs have shown. Sacrifices will have to be made by every generation, so that equality of care and access to that care can be ensured. These conversations also need to take place within the framework of our congregations.

Judaism has always supported the notion that a connection exists between caregiving and maintaining loving, personal relationships. We are reminded in our sacred texts that we are part of a living, organic, spiritual community in which we are all in relationship with one another. We are, the tradition reminds us, responsible for each other's well-being, and that includes responsibility for providing love and support when caregiving is required. In caring for another, we invite in the presence of God, yet this link between caring for loved ones and our relationship with God is often forgotten or denied. As important as being a caregiver is, equally as important is offering emotional, psychological, and spiritual support for the caregiver and the caregiver's family. If we do not "honor and respect" the life of the caregiver, then the person or persons needing care will also suffer.

An increasing number of congregations, Jewish Community Centers, and Jewish Family Service agencies have developed support programs for caregivers. Stress-reduction techniques, such as meditation and yoga, are becoming popular as ways to enable the caregiver to refocus the energy needed to navigate this life stage. One unique idea comes from the website TraditionalKeys.org, which has developed something called a Caregiver's Sanctuary. In a publication that featured this idea, it was noted that "some of our most important work involves restorative rituals for adult children who are caregivers for their parents. Perhaps the most basic of these is the ritual creation of a sanctuary—a peaceful place to go to and return to for restoration and renewal" (Sherman and Weiner 2010, p. 63).

Some congregations, as part of the Union for Reform Judaism's Sacred Aging project, have created special Shabbat services that honor the caregivers within the congregation. Previously we referred to the power of creating and using ritual to sanctify new life stages that occur within this new era of longevity. The challenges associated with being a caregiver are no exception. The following meditation for caregivers seeks to express some of the emotional peaks and valleys that are involved in this new life stage.

All of us at some time in our lives have been caregivers— for parents, children, spouses, friends and each other. Go inside yourself for a moment and relive what it was like to give care to others.

Think of those for whom you have taken responsibility to tend to their needs at a time when they could not.

Now go deeper into yourself and recall the times that others cared for you. Imagine your caregivers in your heart and your mind.

Go even deeper and imagine the love and dedication they felt for you. Take a moment. See it. Feel it. Hear the sounds of their voices.

As we find comfort in the shelter of God, we can find comfort on earth through the loving-kindness of others. (Address and Rosenkranz 2005, p. 47)

Being a caregiver is often thought of as a great source of stress on an individual and a family, and that is often true. Yet there also seem to be some unintended positive consequences that reflect the power and importance of sacred and deep relationships. A study from the University of Michigan, conducted by Stephanie Brown and reported in the journal *Psychological Science*, noted that "if you accounted for the negative impact of stressing over a loved one's illness, that caregiving actually led to a longer life. During the course of the study, people who spent at least 14 hours a week caring for a sick spouse were almost 30 percent less likely to die during the study period than those who spent no time helping . . . A smaller study in the journal *Stroke* came to a similar conclusion. Researchers interviewed 75 people who spent an average of almost 37 hours per week caring for a loved one who had suffered a stroke. A full 90 percent of those interviewed reported that their caregiving enabled them to appreciate life more. Many also reported that it helped them develop a more positive attitude toward life" (Carroll 2009). What accounts for these results? Is it because there is an added meaning, or reason for living, even though it is a burden? Is it because the power of the relationship is so intense that it affirms the power of life and love?

The caregiving revolution is a call for our congregations and agencies to create supportive, relationship-based programs that assist people in this new life stage, which may, and often does, last for years. It is time for every synagogue to create an "ombudsperson" to help clergy in working with families who need support in navigating the labyrinth of insurance forms, plus the myriad benefits and housing options that are available. No one should have to negotiate the life stage of caregiver l'vado (alone). Relationships and community are the healing balm in caring. They can provide the emotional and spiritual support that helps people heal from loss and discover their own strength as they confront the challenges and blessings of honoring and respecting those for whom we care. These challenges, however, often bring us to the point of having to make significant choices. The relationships we have with others and the relationship we develop with God help form a personal spiritual support system that can hold and care for us as we face the often difficult task of making sacred choices for ourselves and for others.

Chapter 6 ————————————————————————————

THE CHOICES
WE MAKE

*I call heaven and earth to witness against you this
day: I have put before you life and death, blessing and
curse. Choose life—if you and your offspring
would live—* DEUTERONOMY 30:19

הַעִדֹתִי בָכֶם הַיּוֹם אֶת־הַשָּׁמַיִם וְאֶת־הָאָרֶץ
הַחַיִּים וְהַמָּוֶת נָתַתִּי לְפָנֶיךָ הַבְּרָכָה וְהַקְּלָלָה
וּבָחַרְתָּ בַּחַיִּים לְמַעַן תִּחְיֶה אַתָּה וְזַרְעֶךָ:

Ha-idoti bachem hayom et hashamayim v'et ha-aretz

hachayim v'hamavet natati l'fanecha hab'rachah v'hak'lalah

uvacharta bachayim l'ma-an tich'yeh atah v'zarecha.

THE BOOK OF DEUTERONOMY CONCLUDES WITH A
famous and often-quoted Torah portion known in the
reading cycle as *Nitzavim*. Like Leviticus 19, it is so
meaningful that we encounter it again every year on Yom Kippur.
The portion has particular relevance for us as we grow older and
seek to live a life of meaning. In *Nitzavim*, Moses stands before the
Israelites for the last time. They are poised to enter the Promised
Land, but Moses will not be leading them across the Jordan. Facing death, Moses reminds the Israelites of all that God has done

for them, their obligations as partners in covenant with God, and the rewards and punishments associated with that covenant. The lesson of this portion is contained in the verses "I call heaven and earth to witness against you this day: I have put before you life and death, blessing and curse. Choose life—if you and your offspring would live—by loving the Eternal your God, heeding God's commands and holding fast to [God]" (Deuteronomy 30:19–20). The phrase *uvacharta bachayim* (choose life) sums up the greatest of challenges that we face as we age. The longevity revolution almost guarantees that either we, personally, or someone in our family, will need to confront decisions regarding issues of chronic illness or end-of-life care. What does it mean, in this context, to choose life? How can we make choices that are embraced and informed by Jewish values and traditions?

When Jewish bioethicists address these questions, they look for the Jewish value at stake. It may be the saving of a life; it may be the commandment to be fruitful and multiply; it may be the preservation of human life in dignity and sanctity that allows for a terminally ill patient to die without pain or discomfort; it may be creating a safe and secure environment for a parent or loved one so that his dignity and sanctity are honored and respected. We look at the value before us and apply it to the particular case or context. The context allows us to see the options available to us. We apply the value to the context, and, in doing so, we can be led to a Jewish-based choice. As many of us know, that choice is sometimes painful. Yet choices need to be made, for even making no choice is choosing a course of action.

We are also reminded that there is no single right choice. Each of us brings to each context our own history, our own universe of experience, our own hopes and fears. Some of us at this moment are facing a decision about how to deal with a difficult situation, diagnosis, or family concern. Under similar circumstances, people may make very different choices. For example, people faced with a debilitating illness may look at their situation in radically different ways. One may curl up and wait to die, choosing to accept what he sees as an inevitable life course. Yet, next door may be another person who sees in a similar diagnosis only a roadblock to living her life. She chooses to embrace life, dealing with the reality of her illness in the context of living and not as the foretaste of dying. Why the difference? How do people from similar backgrounds make such different choices?

I believe that a variety of factors affect how we choose to respond to challenges like these. In developing a theory of decision making, I suggest that three factors, or wild cards, impact how we make a choice. These wild cards are autonomy, technology, and spirituality; they combine to affect how we make sacred decisions in our lives, based on Jewish values. They are approaches that help to make the Deuteronomy texts come alive in our life, for they frame how we choose to search for our own self.

Autonomy

THE FIRST WILD CARD, that of autonomy, refers back, in a way, to the *Un'taneh Tokef* prayer of the High Holy Days, which comments on the façade of control that so many of us like to maintain. This is the liturgy that speaks of God looking down like a shepherd over his flock and making decisions as to who shall live and who shall die. I remember, as a younger rabbi, that this prayer bothered me. When we are younger, many of us harbor the myth of control. *Un'taneh Tokef* is a not-so-gentle reminder that, in the real world, we have control over very little. This is a prayer that, for me, introduces the concept of "mystery." So much remains a mystery to us, and often, at some time in our lives, we begin to accept the mystery of existence and understand that much of life is out of our control.

The concept of autonomy is a particular challenge for contemporary liberal Jews, especially those of us in the United States, who have grown up with a cultural and historical bias toward the value of individual rights and autonomy. We prize independence and fight back when our own independence is threatened. Many of us in the baby boom generation are seeing this firsthand as health issues begin to eat away at the independence of our parents and we fear that we may be looking into our own future as well. We do not do a great job coming to understand that personal autonomy may have a place in life, but to worship it as an ultimate value may, in some cases, be more harmful than good.

But what can we control? Let me suggest a concept of the self that speaks to this issue and reflects just how much autonomy we may have.

Our choices begin with the reality of our genetic code. We are made up of the combined genetic contributions of our parents and their parents and so forth. That genetic legacy is ours, and while science is hard at work deciphering and manipulating it, our DNA generally dictates who we shall be. We first recognize this when we look in the mirror, perhaps in the morning, and all of a sudden see the face of our mother or father. Many of our medical histories are linked to genetics, and it is something over which we have little, if any, control.

In addition to the genetic component, we are also a product of our family of origin. Consider all those messages—both verbal and nonverbal—that our parents sent to us, often while we were still in the womb. Those messages—especially the ones delivered in those first years of life—are powerful determinants of who we will become. How were we treated as children? Were we loved, cared for, challenged, supported, neglected, abused, or ignored? Many of us spend thousands of dollars in therapists' offices trying to free ourselves from the messages we received in those early years. Yet those messages are deeply embedded, hardwired into our psyches and a very strong influence over what and how we choose to live life. Our genetic code and our family of origin underlie who we are, and we can exercise little control over them.

As powerful as these two aspects of our self may be, the final component is what determines the type of person we become. We cannot control our DNA, we cannot control our family of origin or how we were raised in those first formative years. However, we can control how we choose to react to the randomness of our own existence. By this I mean how we choose to deal with the issues and realities that life presents to us. As Moses's speech in Deuteronomy reminds us, what we choose and how we choose affects not only us, but those who come after us. We are not alone, and it is foolish to think that what we do has no impact on others, or has not been influenced by others. Our lives are the story of the choices that we make.

Sandy, a participant in one of our Sacred Aging focus groups is an example of how randomness influences life and how someone chooses to react to events over which she has no control. She spoke about the *it* factor (as in "I never thought *it* could happen to me") and how it has affected her life.

> It is how we act and react to the *it* in our lives that makes us the person we are supposed to be. At least that is what I have learned from all those *it*s. It is because of my deep belief in God, my Jewish upbringing, and the concept of random/chaos/fate that I am finally at peace with my lot in life. I know why I am here.
>
> The first *it* happened in the early '60s when my parents and I were returning from taking some friends to a bus station late one Sunday evening. Within a very short time, while crossing the L.A. River on the 6th Street bridge, a drunk driver, speeding over ninety miles an hour, hit us head-on. My parents were killed and I was in the hospital for seventeen days and out of school for three months. I never thought *it* could happen to me, but *it* did. The devastation to my two brothers and me, my bubie and pa, our family and friends and community was, and still is, beyond words. My parents were 38 years old. . . .
>
> I had a bubie, a Russian-born bubie who lost her parents at a very young age and was raised by her grandparents. She taught all of us that "life goes on, you live for the living, and other people's problems are worse." But, most importantly, she taught us: "You mourn, you cry, you learn to laugh again, and you eat."

. . . I was married before I was twenty, had three beautiful children, lived in a wonderful Jewish community, and was very active. I was living a good life and felt my parents would be happy. My husband of almost twenty years decided he didn't want to be married anymore. I was not prepared for a divorce. . . . I hadn't finished college and was unprepared for the workforce. It was déjà vu all over again. *It* hit me like a ton of bricks.

Soon after this, my bubie died and about a year later, we relocated to the Bay area. I went back to school, completed college, earned a master's degree, bought a small house, and thought my education would put me on easy street. But I have learned that when you make plans, God often laughs, because *it* happened again.

My ex-husband committed suicide. What followed was a lot of lawyers, a lot of creditors, executors, and "This too shall pass." By this time, I had stopped asking *why*. Most often, there are no answers. My bubie often answered that question with "If God didn't tell us why Moses didn't get to Israel, then we just have to have faith and accept that only God knows."

Sandy went on to recount that the *it* continued to impact her life, as she was a victim of the economic downturn, had to sell her house, and had to create a new home with one of her children and grandchildren. Her role is that of caregiver to grandchildren and advisor to her own children. The choices that Sandy made as a result of those random acts of life, her *its*, brought her to where she is today.

> I am a baby boomer bubie, and as God chose for Moses not to enter Israel, God has chosen for me not to have a "normal" life of Sadie, Sadie, married lady with the successful husband and all the trimmings that go with it. My age-old question of why I lived and my parents died has taken me down a path of tragedies, blessings, tears, and laughter. The many "I never thought *it* could happen to me" experiences have brought me where I am today, being there again for children. That is my answer as to why I was left alive in that accident.

An awareness of the randomness of life is captured in the texts of our tradition. The sailors on Jonah's ship draw lots to determine the cause of their catastrophic predicament. There are the random chance meetings of Isaac and Rebecca or Jacob and Rachel. And what of our modern stories? With the random encounter with a person who becomes a partner, or the devastation of an unexpected diagnosis, we see how life changes in an instant. The choices we make in light of these random acts so often shape our own future. Rabbi Edythe Mencher, my colleague in the Union for Reform Judaism's Department of Jewish Family Concerns, sees the challenges of life's randomness in the spinning Chanukah dreidel. Where it lands determines one's stake, or lack thereof, in the game. For many, the spinning dreidel is symbolic of the sense that, too often, we feel as if our own lives are spinning out of control. We are at the mercy of the randomness of life. We spin the dreidel, its final position is totally random, and then we have to act. Randomness is where we live the majority of life. How we choose to respond to these random occurrences determines the type of person we become. It is how we handle the special-needs grandchild, the leaving home of our children, the invitation to engage in an extramarital affair. It is how we choose to deal with the accident that restructures our lives, the illness that forces us to reevaluate our lifestyle and life course. It is in the way we respond to that new job opportunity or new relationship that came out of the blue, just when we thought such opportunities were over. In dealing with these random acts, the centrality of our relationships often comes to the fore. We can derive from them support and caring, guidance, and spiritual and emotional sustenance; and they become even more important as we ourselves grow older and have to deal with more of these random situations.

How we choose to respond to the randomness of life determines if we have a future of holiness or blame. Rabbi Jonathan Sacks writes that when bad things happen, when we are dealt cards we did not expect or want, and our lives change in ways we could not have anticipated, we can choose to see ourselves as the victim or choose to see hope. There are, says Sacks, two questions we can ask. "The first is: 'Why did this happen to me?' The second question is: 'What then shall I do?'" To Sacks, the questions reflect two types of culture: "The first focuses on the past, the second on the future. When I ask, 'Why did this happen?' I see myself as an object. When I ask, 'What then shall I do?' I see myself as a subject. The first is passive, the second active. In the first I search for someone or something to blame. In the second, I accept responsibility. When I do that, a profound human dignity is born"

(Sacks 2005, p. 179). Thus when faced with critical decisions in our lives or the lives of our loved ones, we must understand the limits of our autonomy. We must let go of what we can't control and take responsibility for what we can.

Technology

THE SECOND WILD CARD affecting our decision making is technology. Here is another test of the wild card of autonomy, for the belief that my life and my body are within my control often comes into conflict with both Jewish tradition and the situation before us. The wild card of technology means understanding what we *can* do versus what we *should* do. When we must make choices about the care of a loved one who is entering the final stages of life, we ask questions of ourselves and family and clergy as to how far we should or must go in treatment. We seek guidance from a variety of sources. Must we keep fighting the battle? Are there boundaries that, once crossed, open up different options for treatment? Medical technology is a blessing. But can this blessing ever become a curse?

Our fundamental relationship with God, drawn from Genesis 1 and 2, reminds us that our lives and our bodies are gifts, and we are not free to deal with them or dispose of them as we please. Jewish teachings on health and medicine seek humane decisions, creating interpretations of texts and traditions that hallow human life and the preservation of that human life in dignity and sanctity. Indeed this is the fundamental ethic that governs how Jewish tradition (in all its denominational variations) sees the dance between autonomy and medical technology. In just about every situation now before us that has the wild card of medical technology as an issue, Jewish tradition has found ways to make the end choice one of dignity and sanctity.

We are taught that human life is our most precious value. We can break almost any law in order to save a life. Yet our tradition understands that there may be times when saving and preserving a life may come into conflict with the dignity and sanctity of life. Classic Jewish texts speak of the legal category of *goses*, a term for a person who is moribund and whose death is close at hand. *Close at hand* was understood to be about three days in duration. In our times, given medical technology, we all know that it is possible to maintain a person for quite a lot longer than three days. Contemporary interpretations of *goses* lead us to an understanding that there are times when the dignity and sanctity of our loved one's life are best honored by allowing life's flame to flicker out. That ending must be one of dignity and sanctity, so the use of pain medication to relieve suffering, even if it hastens the impending death, is permitted. When the arsenal of technology has been depleted, when palliative care is the option that best ensures dignity and sanctity, then a boundary has been crossed and different approaches to honoring the value of human life may be invoked. This is why contemporary Jewish thinkers overwhelmingly support palliative and hospice care at the end of life. Remember that the choices associated with these moments are powerful and contain within them deep psychospiritual challenges. As a result, commentators stress the importance of context, assessing each case on its own merits. There is no single template, no single answer for everyone. Contemporary scholars from all denominational streams draw on the richness of our tradition to point up the contextual nature of our choices and the way our tradition embraces the dignity and sanctity of each life, even as it accepts the inevitability of life's passing. See, for example, the following two comments from Progressive and modern Orthodox scholars:

> It is clear in each of these cases, and in others like them, we should do our best to enhance the quality of life and to use whatever means modern science has placed at our disposal for this purpose. We need not invoke "heroic" measures to prolong life, nor should we hesitate to alleviate pain, but we can also not utilize a "low quality" of life as an excuse for hastening death. We cannot generalize about the "quality of life," but must treat each case which we face individually. All life is wonderful and mysterious. The human situation, the family setting and other factors must be carefully analyzed before a sympathetic decision can be reached. (Jacob 1987, p.133)

> Although mercy killing and assisted suicide are opposed in Jewish law and considered as a deliberate hastening of death, Judaism is deeply concerned about pain and suffering. Judaism does not always require physicians to resort to "heroic" measures to prolong life but sanctions the omission of machines and artificial life support systems that only serve to prolong a dying patient's agony, provided, however, that basic care, such as food, good nursing and psychological support is provided. All reputable commentators on the halakhic perspective on terminal care concur that analgesics and narcotics may be given to relieve pain and suffering even if these increase the danger of depressing respiration and of predisposing the patient to contract-

ing pneumonia. Quality of life is a recognized concept in Judaism. (Tendler and Rosner 1993, p. 21)

Because of the wild card of medical technology, and the choices associated with it, an increasing number of congregations and communal agencies are creating annual programs that teach Jewish approaches to end-of-life care and the laws that pertain to advance directives and health care powers of attorney. Judaism has much to teach us about these issues, and there is more agreement among denominations on issues of medical technology than on perhaps any other contemporary issue. Such programs acknowledge that there is a wealth of information available to each of us, but that information does not necessarily equal knowledge. Just because we can choose to do a certain procedure does not automatically mean that we, in certain contexts, should do that procedure. The choices depend on the context of the situation before us. Technology, we are reminded, is neutral. It is how we choose to use it that may determine if it is a blessing or a curse. Thus, from stem cell research to assisted reproduction, from organ donation to allowing the flame of life to flicker out without pain or undue suffering, Jewish choices can be made that incorporate the advances in medical technology and enhance and support our fundamental ethic of the dignity and sanctity of human life.

Spirituality

THE THIRD WILD CARD that impacts the choices we make is our own spirituality. Spirituality is highly personal. It is the way we come to live our belief in a power beyond our own self. It is the practical, day-to-day application of our religious identity. Spirituality is fluid, dynamic, and open to change and adaptation, and, as such, is reflective of our relationship with God. It is, as described by Carol Ochs, "theology walking." In seeking to make sacred decisions, we need to consider not only the implications of those decisions, but also how our own spiritual beliefs affect those decisions. When we make decisions regarding health and end-of-life care, we have to consider what we believe about God, the afterlife, reward and punishment, and how our decisions will affect our understanding of ourselves and those we are close to, in relation to the mystery of life.

There is much discussion in current society about spiritual issues and practice. Indeed baby boomers have been at the heart of the spiritual revolution that is impacting so much of contemporary religious life as our generation continues to seek a sense of personal meaning within the context of the larger universe. In many ways, the spiritual revolution parallels the longevity revolution. Looking back at the last several decades, it seems as if the age of spiritual transition coincides with the baby boom generation, and, as a result, we live in an age of spiritual fluidity. Our own spirituality may not be linked with a formal affiliation with an institution. It is, however, passionately linked with our need to find a sense of our role in life, our place in the universe, and the meaning of our life. This search for spiritual connection increases as we age. We return to seeking the answer to God's *ayecha* in ways that we did not appreciate decades ago when life seemed to stretch out forever. Yet many of us are becoming aware that the clock of our own life span is ticking. In a very practical way, the choices we make as a result of that reality become how we define what spirituality means to us.

So, as important as autonomy and the impact of technology may be in how we make decisions at this point in our lives, our own sense of purpose and meaning, our own spirituality, may be the most powerful factor in how and what we choose to do now and in the future. Why? Because, while automony and technology may be of great importance in medical decision making, it is our own concept of the spiritual that informs all our decisions. Our spirituality reflects our own search for meaning, as nothing else does. Being *m'vakshim* means embracing the mystery of our relationship with that which is beyond our own self and seeing our life, and thus the choices we make in that life, as part of a relationship that transcends our own experience and self. Our spiritual journeys are avenues to the discovery of our own sense of meaning. The journey is dynamic, evolving, and multifaceted, and it is rooted in experience. The mitzvah of living, of engaging the world and life, is the finest laboratory for our evolving spirituality. Melvin A. Kimble and James W. Ellor, writing about Viktor Frankl's work on spirituality and aging, note that Frankl saw life experience as a key in determining meaning and that this search for meaning was a threefold concept. We obtain our sense of meaning through what we give to the world in terms of our own creativity, by what we take from the world in terms of how we experience life, and in the stand we take in the face of life's random acts. "Meaning," they observe, "is not invented but discovered" (Kimble and Ellor 2000, p. 15). The wild card of spirituality is the wild card of our own search for what we stand for in our lives.

The traditional blessing for the study of Torah contains a powerful word. The blessing says *Baruch atah Adonai, Eloheinu Melech haolam, asher kid'shanu b'mitzvotav v'tzivanu la'asok b'divrei Torah*, Blessed is the Eternal, who has commanded us through mitzvot to engage in the study of Torah. What does that word *la'asok* convey? By engaging in a discussion with the text, we create a dialogue that allows the text to speak to us within the context of our own life experience. This dialogue provides guidance and support for our life, opening us to spiritual growth and new avenues for meaning. Carol Ochs captured some of this sense of dialogue and engagement when she wrote that "we aim to talk not *about* God but *to* God, not to analyze texts but to use them to shape our longing" (Ochs 2001, p. 3). The wild card of spirituality becomes the foundation on which our choices can be made—choices that affirm life and sustain and support our own sense of self as we seek our own sense of purpose.

The revolution in spirituality is providing unprecedented opportunities for Jewish institutions to provide outlets for personal growth and discovery. Too often, these institutions have been lax in their desire to do "God talk," to dare to ask us where we see God in our lives and what this relationship means to us. Indeed many of us struggle to articulate the role of religion and spirituality in our lives. Yet we also seek an opportunity to speak about what is important in our lives, what hopes and fears we harbor, and what our legacy will be. The wild card of our own personal spirituality is the discussion of the *why* of our own existence. It is the desire to understand how we can make choices that will bring a sense of meaning to our own existence. It is the desire to understand how, in the midst of a universe that all too often seems to be random, we can make a difference.

The challenge of choice, so elemental in Jewish thought, puts everything we do and are in sacred perspective. As we look back on our lives and contemplate the future, we come to understand that the choices we have made and the choices we will make determine the type of human being we are and shall be. The choices we make determine the quality of the relationships we create and the nature of the community we establish. Moses's speech to the Israelites also reminds us that we do not make those choices in a vacuum. What we choose to do impacts those who come after us. We do not act in isolation. We are part of a greater mystery. We do not act alone.

Chapter 7 ─────────────────────────

FOUR CORE VALUES
FOR OUR FUTURE

*Hillel: Do not separate yourself from the community;
do not be certain of yourself until the day you die;
do not judge another until you are in his position; do not
say of a thing that it cannot possibly be understood,
for ultimately it will be understood; and do not say,
"When I have leisure I will study," for you may
never have leisure.*   PIRKEI AVOT 2:5

AGING IN A SACRED WAY INVOLVES BEING IN RELA-
tionships. How can we translate the ideas contained
within the texts of the theology of relationships
into a formula for our own lives? What matters most is how we
make sense out of our life and our experiences. If "all politics is
local," then let me suggest that all religion—and, to be sure, all
spirituality—is local as well. The impact of our religious affiliation
and our spiritual quotient is measured and appreciated by how it
directly affects each of us. As we look ahead, what we search for is
a way that will make sense for us, a structure of values and beliefs
that we can apply to our life, our relationships, and our experiences that will guide us as we navigate the decades that, we pray,
lie ahead. As members of this emerging and growing cohort of

113

m'vakishim, we want to look forward to a life that has purpose and allows for a legacy of meaning. We seek relationships and community. Can Judaism provide some guidance for creating a future that honors and respects our families, our communities, and our own self? Using the texts of the theology of relationships as a foundation for building a framework for action, let me suggest a model that uses four classic values as a means of translating the Torah texts into our own experience. These four classic Jewish values help give substance and direction to how we can conceptualize the message of sacred aging within the context of our own relationships and our own struggle for meaning. *B'riut* (health), *r'fuah* (healing), *sh'leimut* (wholeness), and *k'dushah* (holiness) can help each of us find meaning in the time that lies before us.

B'riut: *health*

THERE IS A MIDRASHIC STORY about Rabbi Hillel who, after finishing a lesson with his students, walked with them for a while. After some time, Hillel moved to take his leave, and his students asked their teacher where he was going. Hillel replied that he was on his way to perform a religious duty, a mitzvah. Curious, the students asked what that mitzvah was, and Hillel replied that it was to go to the bathhouse to bathe. Hearing this, his students asked if this was a religious duty. To that question, Hillel replied with another question. He asked his students if they were familiar with the fact that people got paid to clean the statues of the king. How much more important was his duty to take care of his body, given that he had been created in the image of God (*Leviticus Rabbah* 34:3).

Perhaps no issue is a bigger concern for us as we age than health. We recognize the importance of keeping up with advances in medicine and maintaining our physical fitness. In one of the more interesting Sacred Aging survey questions, respondents were asked: "As I grow older, I find myself increasingly concerned about . . ." The possible responses included ten major categories (with an eleventh one marked "other"), but the most checked-off selection for both baby boomers and our parents' generation was "health". Judaism sees health as a crucial value, and it is a mitzvah to maintain our health. Health is important because tradition teaches us that health allows us to stand in relationship with God. Tradition understands that if we are sick, we are unable to focus on spiritual matters. Health is a powerful tool in our ability to age in a sacred manner. In his *Mishneh Torah*, Maimonides (a physician himself) reinforced this primary linkage of health and relationship with God when he wrote:

> One who regulates one's life in accordance with the laws of medicine with the sole motive of maintaining a sound and vigorous physique and begetting children to do his work and labor for his benefit is not following the right course. A person should aim to maintain physical health and vigor in order that his soul may be upright, and in a condition to know God. . . . Whoever throughout his life follows this course will be continually serving God, even while engaged in business and even during cohabitation, because his purpose in all he does will be to satisfy his needs so as to have a sound body with which to serve God. Even when he sleeps and seeks repose to calm his mind and rest

his body so as not to fall sick and be incapacitated from serving God, his sleep is service to the Almighty. (Maimonides, *Mishneh Torah, Laws of Proper Behavior* 3:3)

We encounter the importance of health and the proper working of the body every day in the prayer book. We pray every morning that the body functions correctly, knowing that if one thing that is supposed to happen does not we are going to be in trouble. The so-called "veins and arteries" prayer, associated with successfully relieving oneself in the morning, is a daily reminder of just how fragile this thing called health can be and why it figures so prominently in our relationship with God. In the morning service we read:

Blessed are You, Eternal One, our God, Sovereign of the universe, who formed the human being with wisdom, making for us all the vessels and openings of the body. It is revealed and known before the throne of Your glory that if just one of these be opened or one of these be closed, it would be impossible to exist and stand before You. Blessed are You, Eternal One, healer of all flesh, working wonders.

Jewish tradition even anticipated our contemporary emphasis on regular physical exercise. In the twelfth century, Maimonides wrote a treatise in which he correctly identified the need for the body to stay in motion. Exercise should be an essential part of life because it helps relieve stress and helps keep us focused. In his "Preservation of Youth" Maimonides wrote:

Exercise removes the harm caused by most bad habits, which most people have. And no movement is as beneficial, according to physicians, as body movements and exercise. Exercise refers to both strong and weak movements, providing it is movement that is vigorous and affects breathing, increasing it. Violent exercise causes fatigue and not everyone can stand fatigue, or needs it. It is good for the preservation of health to shorten the exercises.

Staying healthy, no matter what condition we are in, is a major thrust of Jewish thought. Yes, even in stages of decline, keeping the body in motion, even in limited ways, is part of a Jewish response to health. Exercise and nutrition are becoming more and more part of how we approach our own aging. The cumulative impact of a health-oriented lifestyle allows us to honor our relationship with God by taking care, as did Hillel, of God's greatest gift to us: our life and our body. Each of us approaches and embraces aging on our own level. We each enter this new life stage at our own pace, and entering it with a reservoir of health can assist us in living a more meaningful life. Aging, in Judaism, is not a disease. It is a life stage that affords us, especially in this age of longevity, untold opportunities for growth and development. Indeed this idea of ongoing development is a cornerstone of the texts that form the theology of relationships. We are reminded that creating or learning something new never has to end.

As essential to our well-being as a healthy body is a healthy attitude. Sometimes it is attitude that can dictate how we see health. Take this response from a man in his sixties who answered as follows a survey question that asked about the times when he realized he was aging: "Yes, I had a stroke when I was only thirty-eight—no cause was found, it was stress-related. I just quit smoking, improved my health habits and became less type A. It certainly made me focus on what's really important. I got married for the second time at age forty, had a second child at forty-one. My stroke was eighteen years ago—a stroke of luck." Two other responders, one in his seventies and one in his eighties, echoed the notion that how we think really does influence how we age: "I thought of myself as maturing. I did not use the word *old* or *aging*. A few months ago I finally realized that I am getting older and I am fine with it. I am diligent in my physical activities and food choices to help me remain as healthy as possible." Likewise: "I have accepted growing older. I work at taking care of my mind and body. I want to be closer to family. I want to remain active in our synagogue and outside activities. I want to share my life more closely with my spouse."

We age as we have lived, and there is no template or standard to which we must conform. The uniqueness of our life experiences help shape the uniqueness of our own aging. We choose our own passage, with those choices built on everything that we have experienced in the years before. According to Sherwin B. Nuland, becoming elderly "is simply entering another developmental phase of life. Like all others, it has its bodily changes, its deep concerns, and its good reasons for hope and optimism. In other words, it has its gains and it has its losses. The key word here is 'developmental.' Unlike most other animals, the human species lives long beyond its reproductive years, and continues to develop during its entire time of existence. We know this to be true of our middle age, a period of life that we consider a gift. We should recognize and also consider as a gift that we continue to develop in those decades that follow middle age. Living longer allows us to continue the process of our development" (Nuland 2007, p. 11).

Nuland also reminds us that, as we grow older, we really do have an increased responsibility to take care of our health. While aging is not a disease (and cannot be cured), as we age we are more susceptible to medical problems. Part of living a life of sacred responsibility, then, is developing a greater awareness of our health: "There comes a stage of life when we can no longer depend on the efficiency of nature's tendency to repair cellular irregularities and preserve physiological balance. As this dependability lessens incrementally throughout the middle years and later, we need gradually to take over the job ourselves" (Nuland 2007, p. 26).

This call for taking responsibility for our own health is a call that goes largely unheard within the organized Jewish community. One of the ways that Jewish communal institutions like synagogues and community centers can become more responsive to this traditional linkage of Judaism and health is to develop text-based programs on health and wellness. I am not talking about the gym and pool at the local JCC (not that there is anything wrong with that). Rather, I am suggesting that synagogues and community centers create curricula that teach the texts of Judaism that speak to the idea of health and then model those teachings within the institution. We are missing a wonderful opportunity to teach the values of health and wellness across generational lines, for given the boomers' understanding of the importance of health, they may, over the next decades, be healthier than their own children and grandchildren.

There is one additional aspect of the value of health that I want to mention. The Jewish medical model is holistic: Mind, body, and spirit are interconnected and do impact one another. Our physical health has a bearing on our mental outlook, and our soul interacts with our mind and body in an ongoing, fluid dialectic. In his book *God, Faith and Health*, Jeff Levin reminds us that health and faith have a direct impact on each other. He cites numerous studies by people like Dr. Harold Koenig of Duke University, Dr. Larry

Dossey and Dr. Stephen G. Post (director of the Center for Medical Humanities, Compassionate Care, and Bioethics at Stony Brook University in New York), showing that faith benefits physical and mental health by validating the human being (think of the interpretations of the *tzadi* in the word *tzelem*) and supporting the ideas of hope, positivism, and optimism. Levin posits an interesting and valuable interpretation of the connections between health and faith and our relationships with God and others. He calls this a *theosomatic medical model*. "There is," he writes, "something more to attaining health than just good genes and the right attitude. That 'something' cannot be accounted for even by the best psychosocial theories or the principles of behavioral medicine. It has to do with engaging in spiritual pursuits and deepening our relationship with God or the eternal, with our own higher self, and with fellow participants in the spiritual quest" (Levin 2001, p. 207). In his way, Levin joins Jewish tradition in maintaining that health is a powerful value as we grow and that social connections are vital in establishing an ecology of health. Thus, the value of *b'riut* encompasses the holistic Jewish approach to mind, body, and spiritual wellness. We acquire strength, sustenance, definition, and meaning from being in relationships; being connected with others; and having a sense of intimacy, care, and love as the cement that binds these relationships. This is part of health, for it adds to the health of the spirit.

R'fuah: healing

IT IS ALMOST IMPOSSIBLE to go to a synagogue now and not hear the prayer for healing. The *Mi Shebeirach* prayer calls on God to grant healing of the body and the soul to those who are ill, as well as asking for blessings on caregivers and those who tend to the sick. New melodies written to the traditional text have found their way into religious services all over the world. Jewish tradition is filled with references to the power and process of healing. In Numbers 12:13, Moses utters what, for some, is the first prayer for healing, invoking God to heal his sister, Miriam (*El nah, r'fanah lah*—God, please heal her). The book of Psalms has, for centuries, been seen as a classic repository of healing prayers. The famous early Chasidic master Rabbi Nachman of Bratzlav identified ten psalms that would bring about healing of body and spirit (16, 32, 41, 42, 59, 77, 90, 105, 137, and 150). Dr. Carol Ochs and Rabbi Kerry Olitzky reference Psalm 119 as a model for creating one's own personal psalm of healing and spiritual guidance by using the Hebrew letters at the start of each stanza and using the Hebrew letters of a person's name (Ochs and Olitzky 1997, pp. 185–99). Traditional blessings have been reintroduced into synagogue liturgies and given prominence as blessings that give voice to particular aspects of healing. For example, the *birkat gomel* blessing is reentering popular usage in many synagogues as a prayer expressing community support for those who have emerged from serious surgery or difficult personal circumstances. I have seen this used in congregations to welcome individuals back into the congregation who have survived cancer treatments or near-fatal accidents. Likewise, the traditional second blessing of the *Amidah* prayer, which touches on the resurrection of the soul, has been used by those who have emerged from the darkness of clinical depression. They now understand what it means to have a soul revived. The *Mi Shebeirach* prayer has been interpreted by families dealing with mental health issues and recast to address those concerns:

May God Who blessed our fathers and mothers, Abraham, Isaac, and Jacob, Sarah, Rebecca, Rachel, and Leah, grant blessed healing to all those members of our congregation and members of our families who struggle with mental illness. May God be with them in their illness and give them patience, hope, and courage. May God so endow their attending physicians and therapists with insight and skill that they may soon be restored to health and vigor of body and mind. May God be with their families, too, and grant them patience, hope, and courage. May God remove their anger and wipe away their feeling of guilt. May God endow them with a full life and with love that they too enjoy health and vigor of body and mind. May God bind up their wounds that they may enjoy many a *simchah* and thank God for the blessing of health. Let us say, Amen.

(Address 2003, pp. 50–51)

An interesting insight into the value system of Judaism is that we pray for healing and not a cure. This perspective recognizes that, in many ways, we are all imperfect and in need of faith, support, and caring. We all must learn to deal with devastating illnesses and life events that change us, our families, and our lives. We may wish to dwell on these past events, living in that land of "if only" or "would have," "could have," or "should have." Yet, we never stand still, as *Lech l'cha* reminds us. Perhaps, then, healing is the ability to deal, in a sacred and meaningful way, with the losses that we all incur as we live our lives. In this way, the key to healing is wisdom: "If wisdom means anything, it means the ability to see through the illusions of youth. That is the most liberating aspect of age. It frees the mind and enlivens the soul" (Roszak 2001, p. 136).

This sense of wisdom is especially relevant to us at this time. Over the past decades we have witnessed the explosion of information available to us. It comes in every form, from cable television to streaming video to endless websites. Commentators have dubbed this "the information age." Yet, despite our surfeit of information, we seem to lack wisdom. Here is where communities and congregations can step up to model behaviors. In every community, certainly in every congregation, there is a wealth of human experience that often is untapped, underused, and often unappreciated. We call this *spiritual capital*, and it is real-life experience that is needed in today's world. It is a shame that so few Jewish communities foster and develop mentoring programs or create panels of elders to guide people or share experiences in everything from business to professions to life lessons. We are part of a generation emerging as elders. Just think of the wisdom drawn from our life experiences that could be put to use within our own communities. Remember, this is not a static concept. We do not "arrive" at a place of wisdom and cease learning and growing. Quite the contrary. We enhance that wisdom by continuing to seek out new experiences and new interpretations of life.

The image of the Torah is quite relevant in this context. Each year we read the same section on assigned weeks. Each year, we bring that past year's experiences to the text, and often we see the text in a new light. We build on what we have experienced, and, with that experience, we pray, will come understanding and wisdom, for part of the excitement of our own aging is the continuing opportunity to learn more about our world and our self: "Wisdom increases with age only for those who never lose their receptiveness to change and to progress within themselves" (Nuland 2007, p. 272). Our own healing is a powerful value to embrace and incorporate into our lives. It is, then, not only a healing from illness and distress, but a healing from the challenges and aggravations of living from which we hope, over time, to learn truth.

This is very reflective of the lessons from Deuteronomy 30 and the important role that choice has in how we heal and live. We often acquire wisdom through living our lives and facing the challenges that life hands us. Again, attitude is crucial when it comes to the steps we take to move forward in life, especially after events or circumstances deal us unexpected challenges. How we choose to handle those random events goes a long way toward creating an ecology of healing and wisdom. I came across a story a while ago that illustrates this point. The story was included as part of a final paper by a student of mine at Hebrew Union College. Marion was taking my class on Sacred Aging and was developing a series of seminars and workshops at a congregation. She wrote a course outline for a series of interactive sessions, called "Making Meaning at Midlife." In the midst of the paper she shared a story. The story's origins seem murky. We could not find where it had originated. It has been published in a variety of places. Its message is one that resonates, however, for many. The famed violinist Itzhak Perlman was giving a concert. Perlman had been afflicted by polio as a child and moving can sometimes be a challenge because he wears leg braces and uses crutches. On this particular night, he moved slowly and took his place onstage. After the welcoming applause died down, he signaled the conductor to begin. At that moment, one of the strings on Perlman's violin broke. He had a choice: replace the string and start the concert over, or continue with just three strings. The silence of the moment was broken when Perlman signaled the conductor to proceed from where they had stopped. He now faced the challenge of finding some of the missing notes on the strings that remained and, when needed, rearranging the music on the spot so the integrity of the piece was maintained. He completed the concert with zest, passion, and artistry. As the final notes sounded, silence greeted the performers, soon after shattered by wild applause, as all in attendance knew that they had witnessed something amazing and rare. As the applause subsided, Perlman raised his bow, asked for quiet, and then said: "You know, sometimes it is the artist's task to find out how much beautiful music you can still make with what you have left."

The challenge of seeking healing, of body or mind or soul, is sometimes learning to live with what still remains viable and valid in our lives. Wisdom may sometimes be the ability to accept what life has given us and move forward playing the notes of our own symphony.

Sh'leimut: wholeness

IN THE *V'AHAVTA* PRAYER we are commanded to love God with all our heart, soul, and might. In other words, our relationship with God encompasses all aspects of our selves. The third value for how we translate the theology of relationships into our own lives is the value of wholeness and completeness. The root of *sh'leimut*, as some may surmise, is the three Hebrew letters that form the basis of the word *shalom: shin, lamed,* and *mem.*

As a core value, *sh'leimut* means that one of the goals of our lives is to achieve a sense of completeness, to feel that things have come together and that the various aspects of our lives are integrated. We become at peace with ourselves. As a life goal, this can be elusive and sometimes transient, but there is a beautiful message here for us. Our lives are never finished becoming. We were created incomplete. Life is a constant movement to answer *ayecha?* The Mussar movement, which focuses on the ethical and mystical elements of Jewish life, reflects this sense of continuing spiritual evolution in search of wholeness. Alan Morinis, founder of the Mussar Institute, writes:

> Sometimes they say that the purpose of Mussar practice is to help us move in a direction of *sh'lemut* (or *sh'lemus*), which translates literally as "wholeness." The great Mussar teacher Rabbi Moshe Chaim Luzatto discusses this notion in his book *Da'at Tevunot* (*Discerning Knowledge*): "The one stone on which the entire building rests is the concept that God wants each person to *complete* himself body and soul . . ." He is telling us that we are created incomplete so that we can complete the work of our own creation. (Morinis 2007, p. 14)

What many boomers are finding is that this work of completing our own creation does not begin to occur until this stage in our lives. And, as is often the case, the randomness of life plays a part in pushing us toward a creative next stage, if we are but open to receive the message. Take, for example, Hope's story:

> At some point in my forties, I was visiting a little gift shop and was entranced by a section set up to celebrate older women. There was a book featuring the poem titled "When I Am an Old Lady I Shall Wear Purple." In that same corner of the gift store, there was Red Hat Society parapher-

nalia displayed, and there was a kitchen magnet with a definition of a crone. I had always believed a crone was an old witch. But, according to the definition, a crone was a wise woman, a revered elder and teacher. At that moment, I became keenly aware of my own mortality and knew I wanted to be a crone when I was an old woman. I didn't know exactly what I would teach, but I had set an internal course for the future.

It was clear to me from an early age that I was meant to be a healer, that I was meant to touch people in some way. But, before I could *truly* discover my purpose, I had to grow into my authentic self.

George Bernard Shaw wrote that "Life isn't about finding yourself, life is about creating yourself." I disagree. First I had to discover my real self, which was buried under all those social masks and adaptations we develop throughout the years to become what we think is acceptable to others. What we lose, unfortunately, is who we are at the core. Finding my own inner terra firma has been the most painful and most wonderful work of my life. The more I began to discover who I truly was, the more I could be myself with others. The more authentic I was with others, the more people responded to me. What's so ironic about this is that we develop all these social masks from childhood on expressly to get more love, approval, and validation. And, yet, the miracle is that when you discover who you really are and let it shine, you attract all you want. Now *that* is the real law of attraction. Once I was able to rediscover who I truly was and live from that space more and more, my work became about creating and developing other aspects of myself.

In our desire to achieve a sense of *sh'leimut* in our own lives, we may need to reorient our feelings and attitudes to what it means to grow older. A tension still exists in our society between viewing aging as the "golden" years or seeing it as the time of decline and infirmity. Thomas R. Cole, in his *Journey of Life* sees the need for baby boomers to create a new social and thus personal view of aging. He calls for a re-visioning of the dualistic view that sees aging as a "good old age of health, virtue, self-reliance and salvation" versus a "bad old age of sickness, sin, dependency, premature death and damnation." Cole states that this either/or dualistic approach to aging gets in the way of a more holistic, spiritual view in which there is no one template for every human being and that aging, like the rest of life, is filled with contradictions and tensions. "Aging, like illness and death, reveals the most fundamental conflict of the human condition: the tension between infinite ambitions, dreams and desires on the one hand, and vulnerable, limited, decaying physical existence on the other—the tragic ineradicable conflict between body and spirit" (Cole 1992, p. 239).

The search for *sh'leimut* is a search for a life that integrates all aspects of our past and our present and one that can support our journey onward. There is work in the acquisition of *sh'leimut*. It is our life's work—coming to understand the place we have in life and the legacy we wish to leave—and it never ends! I think this point is behind the rise within our community of programs that bring groups of older adults and boomers together to discuss their life's journey and to create opportunities for spiritual autobiography or legacy projects. This is nothing more than a contemporary interpretation of the traditional ethical will. The ethical will is based on Genesis 18:19, which states: "For I have singled him out, that he may instruct his children and his household after him to keep the way of *Adonai* by doing what is just and right, in order that *Adonai* may bring about for Abraham what *Adonai* has promised him." From this the custom evolved for individuals to write out a personal statement of beliefs that they would leave to the next generation. This is not a list of stocks and bonds, but a reflection on how to live a life. It is the wisdom of *r'fuah* through the filter of experience in the hope of leaving a statement of *sh'leimut*. Communities are using this idea to reach out to our generation and the one before us. Facilitators use both classic and contemporary texts as thought starters, asking participants to reflect on the text to start the process of writing their own spiritual journey. A popular and powerful contemporary text appears in the Reform movement's High Holy Day prayer book as a meditation before the *Kaddish* prayer on Yom Kippur evening. Look at this prayer/poem and consider how you would respond in attempting to chronicle your own spiritual journey, your search for *sh'leimut* in your life:

> Birth is a beginning
> And death a destination.
> And life is a journey:
> From childhood to maturity
> And youth to age

From innocence to awareness
And ignorance to knowing;
From foolishness to discretion
 And then perhaps to wisdom;
From weakness to strength
Or strength to weakness—
 And often back again;
From health to sickness
 And back, we pray, to health again;
From offense to forgiveness,
From loneliness to love,
From joy to gratitude,
From pain to compassion,
And grief to understanding—
 From fear to faith;
From defeat to defeat to defeat—
 Until, looking backward or ahead,
We see that victory lies
Not at some high place along the way,
But in having made the journey, stage by stage,
 A sacred pilgrimage.
Birth is a beginning
And death a destination.
And life is a journey,
A sacred pilgrimage—
 To life everlasting.

       (Stern 1978, pp. 283–84)

K'dushah: holiness

THE COMBINATION OF *B'RIUT, R'FUAH, AND SH'LEIMUT* leads us to our sense of *k'dushah*, holiness. Here we return to the fundamental relationship that we have in life—that of our relationship with God—and the fundamental question that faces us as *m'vakshim*: what do we wish to achieve in our search for meaning? We know by this time in life that material things are just that—material. They cannot buy happiness or health; they cannot provide us with wisdom or a sense that our existence here on earth means something. As we look forward into the uncharted expanse of our own aging, we come to understand that it is the spiritual aspect of life that provides the texture, the nuance, the quiet sense of our place in life and in the universe. By living a life that reveres health of body, mind, and soul; a life that seeks to understand the context of life's experiences so as to acquire wisdom, and that thus seeks wholeness, unity, and peace, we come to live a life in relationship with the Mystery of all existence. Our pathway to that Mystery is through the relationships we create with others and the interactions we have with them. Through those encounters, we find our self and our God.

What does it mean to live a life of holiness? We will each answer that for ourselves as we struggle to respond to God's *ayecha?* A Sacred Aging survey asked, "Looking forward in your life, what insights, thoughts, or feelings would you like to share as a result of your own life experience?" The answers, obviously, were varied. Yet the themes of relationships, family, giving back, attitude, and acceptance of the blessings of what life has given to each person seemed to run through most of those responses. There was no great difference between the baby boomers and those of the older generation. Marla, a fifty-one-year-old woman from the Midwest, wrote, "I have learned that we all need validation of our lives and while we can give ourselves this (to a point), it is imperative to offer this to one another." This seems to encompass the Jewish value of *kavod*—respect.

Susan, a woman in her sixties from Michigan, reminded us that "life is stranger than 'the soaps.' Nobody could make some of this stuff up. Worrying is rather useless as about 99 percent of what you worry about never happens and what bad stuff does happen is usually something you'd never ever think of." Susan also reminded us that, as a result of seeing so many people with whom she was close deal with significant mental and physical health issues, she has learned "to be grateful for my own personal blessings and take each day one step at a time." A great number of the people who responded to the Sacred Aging survey also wrote that their own aging and life experiences have taught them that part of holiness is being grateful for the blessings that they enjoy. Attitude can be so important, as one Florida woman suggested when she reminded us that to her "life is a journey of surprises. You have to go with the flow with things that cannot be changed. Celebrate each day and always see that glass half full."

We can learn from the challenges that life throws at us, as another Sue remarked:

> I have often gone to the well of my faith to draw sustenance throughout my life. My father died when I was twelve; my mother when I was twenty-three. . . . I had a heart attack at forty-three; a triple bypass at fifty-three . . . now, at fifty-five, I continue to draw on the never-ending flow of

strength I get from my belief. I neither fear nor welcome death. I simply accept the rhythm of my existence. I see the beginning and the end and am content with what is. Don't sweat the small stuff. Don't be so critical of yourself. Don't let what you believe others are thinking affect you so much. In the end, what you have given in money is not as important as what you've given in love.

We return to the power of love and the need for connection and relationships. Is this the true path to meaning and holiness? How many of us know people who search not for holiness or meaning, but for those elusive concepts of happiness and success? Happiness and success seem to have become commodities that, if we just try hard enough or acquire enough "stuff," they will be ours. But it is a mistake to see both happiness and success as defined from without, as opposed to within our soul. There are many who appear to the outside world happy and successful, yet whose souls are empty and *l'vado*. This outwardly motivated search can often become a vain and false crusade. Happiness and success are not commodities that can be "purchased." They are intensely personal and are acquired over time by our ability to give and receive love and be with others in relationship and community. Psychologist Dr. Dan Gottlieb seemed to echo what Sue was writing about when he reminded me that "the pursuit of happiness is a surefire way to be miserable." Gottlieb reinforced the idea that so many of the people who spoke to us in workshops and who responded to our survey mentioned that meaning, or happiness, or holiness, was attained through being with others, living and doing for others, and being part of the community: "The more your life is about others, compassion for others, love for others, the healthier you will be

. . . caring for others is life-altering, life-sustaining" (Gottlieb 2009). Gottlieb echoed Viktor Frankl, who wrote from his Holocaust experience:

> Don't aim at success—the more you aim at it and make it a target, the more you are going to miss it. For success, like happiness, cannot be pursued; it must ensue, and it only does so as the unintended side effect of one's personal dedication to a cause greater than oneself or as a by-product of one's surrender to a person other than oneself. Happiness must happen, and the same holds for success: you have to let it happen by not caring about it. I want you to listen to what your conscience commands you to do and go on to carry it out to the best of your knowledge. Then you will live to see that in the long run—in the long run, I say—success will follow you precisely because you had forgotten to think of it. (Frankl 1959, pp. 16–17)

The value of *k'dushah*, then, focuses us outward, not inward, and brings us toward a life of meaning by allowing us to experience the sacred in the daily act of living.

In the end, a sacred approach to our own aging returns to how we will choose to answer God's question, *ayecha*? If we recognize and celebrate our fundamental relationship with God, we are affirmed in our own sense of worth and uniqueness. For that we may rely more on our instincts and our feeling of self-worth than on any great formula. Faith in our self seems to be the first step in creating a successful approach to our aging. This is not the worship of self, but the feeling that this is the time in our lives when we can embrace our unique selves. Accepting our self deepens our relationships with others. There is no need to "be" someone we are not, and this honesty of acceptance can lead to more enhanced and powerful relationships with others. We can embrace the values of health, healing, wholeness, and holiness as standards on which we can hang our thoughts and our actions. Yet it still comes down to how we choose to live our lives and how we choose to be in relationship with our God and with our fellow human beings, how we choose to answer *ayecha*. Two of my oldest friends, Larry and Gail, have lived a wonderful life of close and meaningful relationships. Their own family is a reflection of the demographics of the contemporary Jewish family. They have had to deal with the premature death of a parent, interfaith marriage, chronic illness afflicting other parents, family marital disruption, and the birth of a grandchild with serious medical challenges. Their relationship has been tested and the stresses of work and the world have tried their souls. Yet when we discuss the search for meaning as we age, they look forward to the future, despite all the issues that have confronted them. As many of the people we met with pointed out, they recognize that life offers no guarantees, no magical manual of how to live without some pain and distress. We worry that our children may not be able to enjoy a lifestyle as economically sound as ours. We worry that, despite all the advances in technology and the promises of scholars and pundits, we may not be that different from other generations after all. Consequently, it is not surprising that we are becoming more engaged with our own spiritual journeys. As Larry reminded me when I asked him to share some insight based on his experience, "Enjoy each stage of life: Each has its own insights, pleasures, and rewards. Don't let the fork in the road get you lost. A warm smile and concern for others brings much to one's soul."

The celebration of the miracle of our own life sets the tone for how we choose to see our future. The randomness of life exacts challenges on us that test our ability, our faith, and our relationships. Yet all of us find ways of choosing how to live. Judaism, our texts, and our traditions provide a foundation for these choices. They teach an embrace of faith, trust, hope, love, and choice, plus they give us permission to change and adapt, to doubt and question. As images of the Divine, we, each in our own way, struggle to find what gives us pleasure, what provides meaning for us, and what defines our legacy. That struggle, that challenge defines who we are and how we shall age. It is a struggle that, as with all of life, is filled with the tension of duality: of pain and pleasure, of hope and disappointments, of dreams fulfilled and dreams lost, of the small quiet victories that take place every day whose impact may not be realized for years. Living each day, surrounded and supported by friends and family, precious relationships of life and memory, helps shape who we will become. The challenges of life will continue.

At the end of the Woody Allen movie *Crimes and Misdemeanors*, there is a wonderful wedding scene. We see the guests, many of whom we have observed during the film struggling with serious moral and ethical challenges, some of which remain unresolved. As the scene plays on, and we realize that, as in life, not everything is ending with a satisfactory conclusion, the narrator's voice reminds us:

> We are all faced throughout our lives with agonizing decisions, moral choices. Some are on a gramd scale. Most of these choices are on lesser points. But, we define ourselves by the choices we have made. We are, in fact, the sum total

of our choices. Events unfold so unpredictably, so unfairly, human happiness does not seem to have been included in the design of cration. It is only we, with our capacity to love, that give meaning to the indifferent universe. And yet, most human beings seem to have the ability to keep trying and even to find joy from simple things, like thier family, their work, and from the hope that future generations might understand more.

We are emboldened and supported by the little victories of our lives. This search for meaning begins with each of our souls. It is not dependent on economic riches or social status or the number of "toys" we amass on our way to the grave. Our sense of worth is given to us as a birthright. Our sense of meaning is defined not by what we have or what we have attained, but by how we choose to live this gift called life. We achieve meaning and purpose through these choices and in the context of the relationships that we create and foster. In our struggle to not be *l'vado*, we are defined by the love we have, and the love we give. Love, connection, intimacy, friends, family, community—these will be our guide in this next stage of life. And if you need confirmation of this, just look into the eyes of a grandchild. Look deeply and see yourself, your legacy, your love.

The paradox of our existence is that we are born to die. The lifelong search for the answer to the question of *ayecha* is the task of our own journey. We do not know what tomorrow will bring. There is no tried-and-true template that will allow us to successfully navigate what we cannot control. The sacred texts of Judaism, as presented here, can offer a guide for living and a pathway by which we can see our faith and tradition as supportive of a life of growth, learning, transformation, and creativity, all embraced by the centrality of relationships. Yet each of us, as unique individuals, will choose our own paths.

In making our choices, let me close with one final text—one of my favorites—that reminds us of a path that, when all else seems confusing, brings us back to truth.

In a place where no one acts like a human being, strive to be a human being. (*Pirkei Avot* 2:6)

B'makom sh'ain anashim, hishtadel l'hiyot ish.

We have each been created as *tzelem Elohim*, unique individuals of worth and dignity, having the potential to bring our own humanity into the world so that we find meaning in this most exciting of mysteries: human life. Let us not be afraid to *lech l'cha*, to go forth into our future.

References

Address, Richard F., ed. 2003. *R'fuat HaNefesh: Caring for the Soul*. New York: UAHC Press.

Address, Richard F., and Andrew L. Rosenkranz. 2005. *To Honor and Respect*. New York: URJ Press.

Association of Jewish Family and Children's Agencies. 2008. "Engaging Baby Boomers in JFS and Other Jewish Community Volunteer Agencies," www.ajfca.org/babyboomer/report.

Atchley, Robert C. 2009. *Spirituality and Aging*. Baltimore: Johns Hopkins University Press.

Bazeley, Phil. 2009. "Ritual Commemorating Becoming an *Aguneh/Agunah* Due to Illness." Hebrew Union College–Jewish Institute of Religion.

Berman Jewish Policy Archive. 2010. "Baby Boomers, Public Service and Minority Communities."

Bleich, J. David. 1999. "Can There Be Marriage without Marriage?" *Tradition* 33, no. 2 (Winter): 39–49.

Buber, Martin. 1998. *The Way of Man*. Secaucus, NJ: Citadel Press/Carol Publishing.

Bulka, Reuven P. 1993. *Chapters of the Sages*. Northvale, NJ: Jason Aronson.

Butler, Robert. 2008. *The Longevity Revolution*. New York: Public Affairs.

Carroll, Linda. 2009. "Caring for Ill, Elderly Has Reward—Longer Life." MSNBC.com (May 5).

Chernick, Michael. 1987. "Who Pays? The Talmudic Approach to Filial Responsibility." In *That You May Live Long*, edited by Hara Person and Richard F. Address. New York: URJ Press.

Cohen, Norman J. 1998. *Voices from Genesis*. Woodstock, VT: Jewish Lights Publishing.

———. 2003. *Hineni in Our Lives*. Woodstock, VT: Jewish Lights Publishing.

Cohen, Steven M. 2010. Foreword to *Baby Boomers, Public Service and Minority Communities: A Case Study of the Jewish Community in the United States*, by Elcott, David M., New York: Research Center for Leadership in Action and Berman Jewish Policy Archive, NYU Robert F. Wagner Graduate School.

Cole, Thomas R. 2004. "After the Life Cycle. The Moral Challenges of Later Life." In *Midrash and Medicine*, edited by William R. Cutter, 137–59 Woodstock, VT: Jewish Lights Publishing.

———. 1992. *The Journey of Life*. Cambridge, UK. Cambridge Univeristy Press.

Dominus, Susan. 2004. "Life in the Age of Old, Old Age." *New York Times Magazine* (February 22): 29–30.

Driver, Tom F. 1991. *The Magic of Ritual*. San Francisco: HarperSanFrancisco.

Feinstein, Edward, ed. 2007. *Jews and Judaism in the 21st Century*. Woodstock, VT: Jewish Lights Publishing.

Frankl, Viktor. 1959. *Man's Search for Meaning*. Boston: Beacon Press.

Friedan, Betty. 1993. *The Fountain of Age*. New York: Simon & Schuster.

Friedman, Dayle A. 2011. "The Journey of Later Life: Moses as Our Guide." In *Midrash and Medicine*, edited by William R. Cutter, 160–76. Woodstock, VT: Jewish Lights Publishing.

———. 2003. "Beyond Guilt: What We Owe Aging Parents." In *That You May Live Long*, edited by Hara Person and Richard F. Address, 78–89. New York: URJ Press.

Gafni, Marc. 2001. *Soul Prints*. New York: Fireside.

Goldberg, Dick. 2009. *Focus on Faith* (radio interview), WNJC-AM, Sewell, NJ. (April).

Gordis, Daniel. 1995. *God Was Not in the Fire*. New York: Scribner.

Gottlieb, Dan. 2009. *Focus on Faith* (radio interview), WNJC-AM, Sewell, NJ. (March 10).

Heschel, Abraham Joshua. 1955. *God in Search of Man*. New York: Farrar, Straus and Giroux.

———. 1965. *Who Is Man?* Stanford, CA: Stanford University Press.

———. 1966. *The Insecurity of Freedom*. New York: Farrar, Straus and Giroux.

———. 1972. *The Insecurity of Freedom*. New York: Schocken Books.

———. 1996. *Moral Grandeur and Spiritual Audacity*. New York: Farrar, Straus and Giroux.

Hollis, James. 2005. *Finding Meaning in the Second Half of Life*. New York: Gotham.

Imber-Black, Evan, and Janine Roberts. 1992. *Rituals for Our Times*. New York: HarperCollins.

Jacob, Walter. 1987. "Quality of Life and Euthanasia." In *Contemporary American Reform Responsa*, 138–40 New York: CCAR Press.

Jones, James. 1995. *In the Middle of This Road We Call Our Life*. New York: HarperCollins.

Kimble, Melvin A., and James W. Ellor. 2000. *Viktor Frankl's Contribution to Spirituality and Aging*. Binghamton, NY: Haworth Press.

Kurtz, Ernest, and Katherine Ketcham. 1992. *Spirituality of Imperfection*. New York: Bantam.

Langer, Ruth. 1998. "Honor Your Father and Mother: Caregiving as a Halachic Responsibility." In *That You May Live Long*, edited by Hara Person and Richard F. Address, 113–26. New York: URJ Press.

Levin, Jeff. 2001. *God, Faith, and Health*. New York: John Wiley and Sons.

McArdle, Megan. 2008. "No Country for Young Men." *The Atlantic* 301, no. 1 (January/February).

Moody, Harry R., and David L. Carroll. 1997. *The Five Stages of the Soul*. New York: Doubleday.

Morinis, Alan. 2007. *Everyday Holiness*. Boston: Trumpeter Books.

Mundy, Alicia. 2009. "Of Love and Alzheimer's: When Caregivers Find New Companions, Is It Adultery?" *Wall Street Journal* (November 3): D4.

Nouwen, Henri J. M. 2005. *The Dance of Life: Weaving Sorrows and Blessings into One Joyful Step*, edited by Michael Andrew Ford. Notre Dame, IN: Ava Maria Press.

Nuland, Sherwin B. 2007. *The Art of Aging*. New York: Random House.

Ochs, Carol. 1994. *Song of the Self*. Harrisburg, PA: Trinity Press International.

————. 2001. *Our Lives as Torah*. San Francisco: Jossey-Bass.

Ochs, Carol, and Kerry M. Olitzky. 1997. *Jewish Spiritual Guidance*. San Francisco: Jossey-Bass.

Pausch, Randy. 2008. *The Last Lecture*. New York: Hyperion.

Potok, Chaim. 1967. *The Chosen*. New York: Ballantine Books.

Pruchno, Rachel A., and Michael A. Smyer. 2007. *Challenges of an Aging Society*. Baltimore: Johns Hopkins University Press.

Remen, Rachel Naomi. 1996. *Kitchen Table Wisdom*. New York: Riverhead Books.

————. 2000. *My Grandfather's Blessings*. New York: Riverhead Books.

Robb, Thomas A. 1994. "Religious Rituals for Life Stage Events." In *Aging and Spirituality: Forum on Religion, Spirituality and Aging Newsletter*, no. 4 (Winter).

Roof, Wade Clark. 1993. *A Generation of Seekers: The Spiritual Journeys of the Baby Boom Generation*. San Francisco: HarperCollins.

Rosenblatt, Naomi. 1995. *Wrestling with Angels*. New York: Delacorte Press.

Roszak, Theodore. 2001. *Longevity Revolution: As Boomers Become Elders*. Berkeley, CA: Berkeley Hills Books.

Sacks, Jonathan. 2005. *To Heal a Fractured World*. New York: Schocken Books.

Schulweis, Harold M. 1990. *In God's Mirror*. Jersey City, NJ: KTAV Publishing.

Sherman, Andrea, and Marsha Weiner. 2010. "When It's Time for Dad to Give Up the Keys." *Spirituality and Health* (July/August).

Soloveitchik, Joseph. 1965. *The Lonely Man of Faith*. New York: Doubleday.

Stern, Chaim, ed. 1978. *Gates of Repentance*. New York: CCAR Press.

Tendler, Moshe D., and Fred Rosner. 1993. "Quality and Sanctity of Life in the Talmud and the Midrash." *Tradition* 28, no. 1 (Fall).

Twerski, Abraham J. 2009. *A Formula for Proper Living*. Woodstock, VT: Jewish Lights Publishing.

Viorst, Judith. 1986. *Necessary Losses*. New York: Simon & Schuster.

Wolfe, Alan. 2003. *The Transformation of American Religion*. New York: Free Press.

Yalom, Irvin D. 2008. *Staring at the Sun*. San Francisco: Jossey-Bass.

Zornberg, Avivah Gottlieb. 1995. *Genesis: The Beginning of Desire*. Philadelphia: Jewish Publication Society.